KETCHUP VOCA

LEVEL
3 1

i-Scream edu

영어 공부의 핵심은 단어입니다.

케찹보카로
영어 단어 실력을 키우고,
상위 1% 어휘력을
따라잡아 보세요!

케찹보카 친구들

만화 스토리
친구들의 좌충우돌 일상이 그려진
재미있는 만화를 보며
단어 뜻을 배우고,
문장에 어떻게 활용되는지
알아볼 수 있어요!

Dennis	엉뚱하고 낙천적인 성격의 자유로운 영혼! 예측 불가에, 공부에도 관심이 없지만, 운이 좋아 뭘 해도 잘 풀린대요.
Rod	인내심이 크고 생각도 깊은, 다정다감 엄친아! 개구쟁이 쌍둥이 누나, 애완묘 루나가 있어 혼자 있는 것보단 함께 하는 것을 좋아해요.
Kiara	노래를 좋아하는 사교성의 아이콘! 솔직하고 모든 일에 적극적이지만, 금방 사랑에 빠지는 짝사랑 전문가래요.
Sally	논리적이고 긍정적인 모범생! 친구들과 장난도 많이 치지만, 호기심이 많아 관심 분야에 다양한 지식을 갖고 있어요.
Mong	친구들이 궁금한 것이 있을 때 나타나는 해결사! 너무 아는 것이 많아서 어느 별에서 왔는지 궁금하기도 해요.

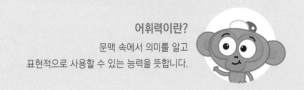

Know　　**Exercise**　　**Think**　　**Check**　　**Habit**

KETCH UP

망각 제로 단어 기억하기 습관으로
기억 장기화

게임으로 즐겁게 리뷰하고 테스트로 더블 체크

만화 스토리 〉 단어 〉 문장 순으로
단어 의미를 이해하며 모국어처럼 습득

이미지 연상 쓰기 연습으로 실제 단어 활용, 적용

주제별로 초등 필수 & 고난도 단어 학습하며
상위 1% 단어 마스터

KETCHUP makes you Catch up.

3

체계적인 4 Steps 시스템으로 학습 완성!

	Step 1	Step 2	Step 3	Step 4
Day 1~4				
Day 5				

Step 1

Warm up 망각 제로＆스토리 단어 이해로 학습 준비하기

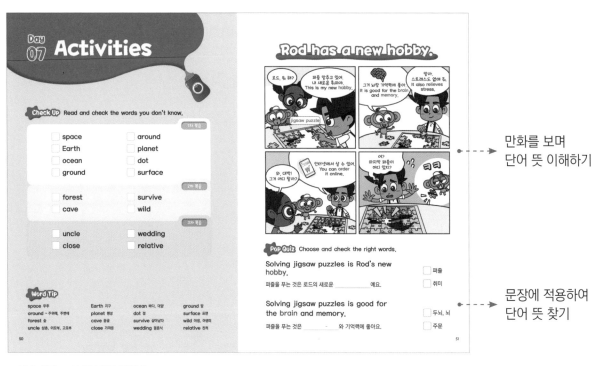

만화를 보며
단어 뜻 이해하기

문장에 적용하여
단어 뜻 찾기

※ 망각 제로는 p10에서 확인하세요!

4

Catch up 듣고, 말하고, 읽고, 쓰며, 상위 1% 단어 따라잡기

QR 찍어 단어 듣고 따라 말하기 ▶ 케찹병을 색칠하며 3번 반복하기

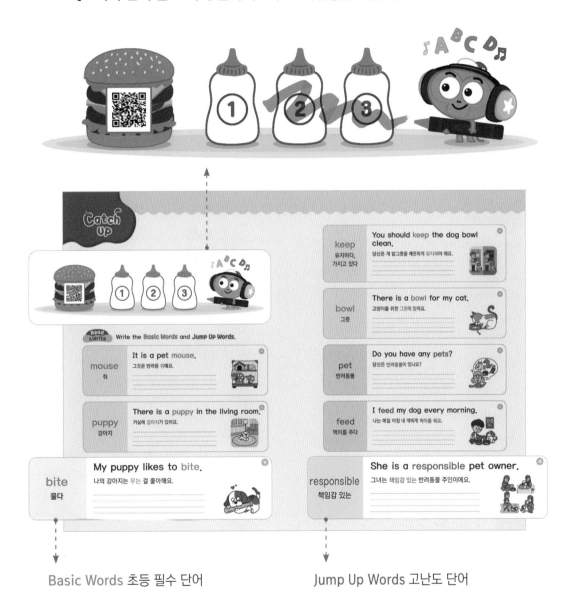

Basic Words 초등 필수 단어   Jump Up Words 고난도 단어

품사 기호

v verb (동사)		**adv** adverb (부사)		**conj** conjunction (접속사)	
n noun (명사)		**prep** preposition (전치사)		**pron** pronoun (대명사)	
a adjective (형용사)		**det** determiner (한정사)		**num** numeral (수사)	

케찹보카와 함께
상위 1% CATCH UP!

Step 3

Skill up 두뇌 자극 이미지 연상 학습으로 실력 강화하기

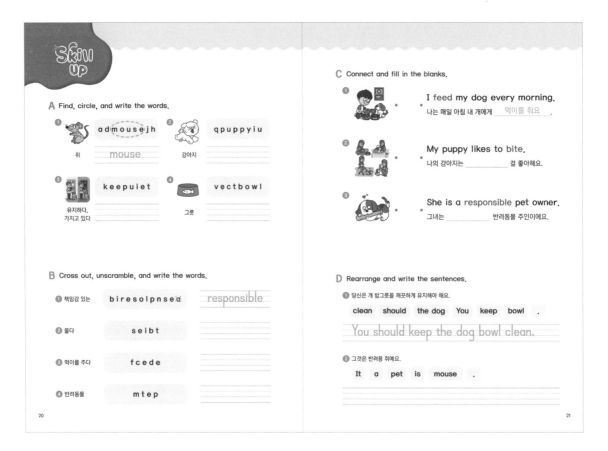

Skill up

A Find, circle, and write the words.

① 쥐 admousejh → mouse
② 강아지 qpuppyiu
③ 유지하다, 가지고 있다 keepuiet
④ 그릇 vectbowl

B Cross out, unscramble, and write the words.

❶ 책임감 있는 biresolpnseα → responsible
❷ 물다 seibt
❸ 먹이를 주다 fcede
❹ 반려동물 mtep

C Connect and fill in the blanks.

① I feed my dog every morning.
나는 매일 아침 내 개에게 먹이를 줘요 .

② My puppy likes to bite.
나의 강아지는 _____ 걸 좋아해요.

③ She is a responsible pet owner.
그녀는 _____ 반려동물 주인이에요.

D Rearrange and write the sentences.

❶ 당신은 개 밥그릇을 깨끗하게 유지해야 해요.
clean should the dog You keep bowl .
You should keep the dog bowl clean.

❷ 그것은 반려용 쥐예요.
It a pet is mouse .

20

21

유형 1
이미지 연상을 통해
단어 완성하기

유형 2
우리말에 맞춰
스펠링 배열하여
단어 쓰기

유형 3
이미지와 문장을
연결하여
단어 뜻 이해하기

유형 4
배운 단어 적용하여
문장 완성하여 쓰기

Wrap up 게임과 최종 평가를 통해 단어 학습 마무리하기

쉬어가기

다양한 유형의 재미있는 게임하며 단어 복습하기!

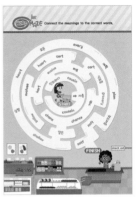 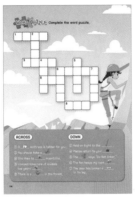  

Word Maze	Word Puzzle	Word Search 1	Word Search 2
알맞은 스펠링으로 이뤄진 단어를 따라가 미로 찾기	주어진 문장에 알맞은 단어를 쓰며 퍼즐 완성하기	힌트를 보고 알맞은 그림을 찾아 쓰기 연습하기	다양한 알파벳 속 배운 단어를 찾아 쓰기 연습하기

복습&테스트

지금까지 배운 단어 정리하고, 테스트로 최종 점검!
뜯어서 쓰는 나만의 단어장까지!

Study Planner & Contents

Part 1

FINISH

START

망각 제로란?

> 망각 제로는
> 학습 주기를 활용해서 복습하는 거야.

> 지난번에 공부했던 단어 중에
> 아는 것과 모르는 것을 확인해 볼 수 있겠네!

Day 07 Activities

Check Up Read and check the words you don't know.

1차 복습
- [ ] space
- [ ] Earth
- [ ] ocean
- [ ] ground
- [ ] around
- [ ] planet
- [ ] dot
- [ ] surface

2차 복습
- [ ] forest
- [ ] cave
- [ ] survive
- [ ] wild

3차 복습
- [ ] uncle
- [ ] close
- [ ] wedding
- [ ] relative

Check Up

복습 주기에 맞춰 반복 학습하기

1차 복습	1일 전 공부한 단어
2차 복습	3일 전 공부한 단어
3차 복습	7일 전 공부한 단어

Pop Quiz Choose and check the right words.

Solving jigsaw puzzles is Rod's new hobby.
퍼즐을 푸는 것은 로드의 새로운 _____ 예요.
- [ ] 퍼즐
- [ ] 취미

Solving jigsaw puzzles is good for the brain and memory.
퍼즐을 푸는 것은 _____ 와 기억력에 좋아요.
- [ ] 두뇌, 뇌
- [ ] 주문

Word Tip

space 우주 Earth 지구 ocean 바다, 대양 ground 땅
around – 주위에, 주변에 planet 행성 dot 점 surface 표면
forest 숲 cave 동굴 survive 살아남다 wild 야생, 야생의
relative 친척

Word Tip

정확한 단어 뜻 확인하기

" 우리 같이
망각 제로 학습해 보자 "

※ 망각 제로는 [DAY 02]부터 시작합니다.

My aunt is getting married!

POP Quiz Choose and check the right words.

It's Dennis's aunt's wedding day.

데니스 고모의 _____ 날이에요.

All the close relatives gathered.

_____ 친척들이 모두 모였어요.

☑ 결혼식

☐ 친척

☐ 가까운

☐ 정중한

 **Listen, say, and color.**

Read &Write Write the **Basic Words** and **Jump Up Words**.

grandfather
할아버지

I go fishing with my grandfather.
나는 할아버지와 함께 낚시하러 가요.

grandfather

aunt
이모, 고모, 숙모

I go shopping with my aunt.
나는 이모와 함께 쇼핑하러 가요.

uncle
삼촌, 이모부,
고모부

I go camping with my uncle.
나는 삼촌과 함께 캠핑을 가요.

close
가까운

My house is close to his house. *a*

우리 집은 그의 집과 가까워요.

_____
_____
_____

wedding
결혼식

Today is my uncle's wedding day. *n*

오늘은 나의 삼촌의 결혼식이에요.

_____
_____
_____

relative
친척

He is my relative. *n*

그는 나의 친척이에요.

_____
_____
_____

declare
선언하다

They declared their love for each other. *v*

그들은 서로에 대한 사랑을 선언했어요.

_____
_____
_____

formal
격식을 차린, 정중한

My uncle is wearing a formal suit. *a*

나의 삼촌은 격식 있는 정장을 입고 있어요.

_____
_____
_____

A Choose and write the words.

> grandfather   aunt   uncle

1 ___uncle___

삼촌, 이모부, 고모부

2 _____

할아버지

3 _____

이모, 고모, 숙모

B Choose and write the words.

> close   wedding   relative   declare

1 | 결혼식 | ___wedding___ | _____ |

2 | 선언하다 | _____ | _____ |

3 | 가까운 | _____ | _____ |

4 | 친척 | _____ | _____ |

C Unscramble and complete the sentences.

1

그는 나의 친척이에요.

r a l e t v i e

He is my _____relative_____.

2

나는 이모와 함께 쇼핑하러 가요.

u n a t

I go shopping with my _____.

3

나는 삼촌과 함께 캠핑을 가요.

e n l u c

I go camping with my _____.

D Choose and complete the sentences.

wedding	formal	declared

1 그들은 서로에 대한 사랑을 선언했어요.

They ____declared____ their love for each other.

2 나의 삼촌은 격식 있는 정장을 입고 있어요.

My uncle is wearing a _____ suit.

3 오늘은 나의 삼촌의 결혼식이에요.

Today is my uncle's _____ day.

Day 02 Raising Pets

Check Up Read and check the words you don't know.

- [ ] grandfather
- [ ] aunt
- [ ] uncle
- [ ] close
- [ ] wedding
- [ ] relative
- [ ] declare
- [ ] formal

※ **망각 제로!** 1일 전 학습한 단어를 복습해요.

Word Tip

grandfather 할아버지	**aunt** 이모, 고모, 숙모
wedding 결혼식	**relative** 친척

uncle 삼촌, 이모부, 고모부   **close** 가까운
declare 선언하다   **formal** 격식을 차린, 정중한

Kiara wants to have a pet.

Pop Quiz Choose and check the right words.

Kiara wants to have a pet.

키아라는 _____을 키우고 싶어요.

- [ ] 반려동물
- [ ] 그릇

Dennis would have to feed and walk a dog every day.

데니스는 강아지를 매일 _____, 산책도 시켜 줘야 해요.

- [ ] 유지하다
- [ ] 먹이를 주다

Listen &Say Listen, say, and color.

Read &Write Write the Basic Words and Jump Up Words.

mouse 쥐	**It is a pet mouse.** ⓝ 그것은 반려용 쥐예요.

puppy 강아지	**There is a puppy in the living room.** ⓝ 거실에 강아지가 있어요.

bite 물다	**My puppy likes to bite.** ⓥ 나의 강아지는 무는 걸 좋아해요.

18

keep
유지하다,
가지고 있다

You should keep the dog bowl clean. (v)

당신은 개 밥그릇을 깨끗하게 유지해야 해요.

_____
_____
_____

bowl
그릇

There is a bowl for my cat. (n)

고양이를 위한 그릇이 있어요.

_____
_____
_____

pet
반려동물

Do you have any pets? (n)

당신은 반려동물이 있나요?

_____
_____
_____

feed
먹이를 주다

I feed my dog every morning. (v)

나는 매일 아침 내 개에게 먹이를 줘요.

_____
_____
_____

responsible
책임감 있는

She is a responsible pet owner. (a)

그녀는 책임감 있는 반려동물 주인이에요.

_____
_____
_____

Skill Up

A Find, circle, and write the words.

1 쥐

admousejh

mouse

2 강아지

qpuppyiu

_____

3 유지하다, 가지고 있다

keepuiet

_____

4 그릇

vectbowl

_____

B Cross out, unscramble, and write the words.

1 책임감 있는

biresolpnsex

responsible

2 물다

seibt

_____

3 먹이를 주다

fcede

_____

4 반려동물

mtep

_____

C Connect and fill in the blanks.

1

I feed my dog every morning.

나는 매일 아침 내 개에게 ___먹이를 줘요___ .

2

My puppy likes to bite.

나의 강아지는 _____ 걸 좋아해요.

3

She is a responsible pet owner.

그녀는 _____ 반려동물 주인이에요.

D Rearrange and write the sentences.

1 당신은 개 밥그릇을 깨끗하게 유지해야 해요.

| clean | should | the dog | You | keep | bowl | . |

You should keep the dog bowl clean.

2 그것은 반려용 쥐예요.

| It | a | pet | is | mouse | . |

Day 03 Weight & Body Image

Check Up Read and check the words you don't know.

1차 복습

- ☐ mouse
- ☐ puppy
- ☐ bite
- ☐ keep
- ☐ bowl
- ☐ pet
- ☐ feed
- ☐ responsible

※ **망각 제로!** 1일 전 학습한 단어를 복습해요.

Word Tip

mouse 쥐   puppy 강아지   bite 물다   keep 유지하다, 가지고 있다

bowl 그릇   pet 반려동물   feed 먹이를 주다   responsible 책임감 있는

How can I lose weight?

 **Pop Quiz** Choose and check the right words.

Sally is going to lose weight.

샐리는 살을 _____ 거예요.

☐ 줄다, 잃다

☐ 얻다, 늘리다

Dennis said, "Eat enough and exercise!"

" _____ 먹고 운동하자" 라고 말했어요.

☐ 날씬한

☐ 충분한

23

 **Listen, say, and color.**

 Write the Basic Words and Jump Up Words.

---

thin
마른, 얇은

He is tall and thin.
그는 마르고 키가 커요.

_____

- - - - - - - - - - - -

_____

_____

ⓐ

---

slim
날씬한

Exercising can help you stay slim.
운동은 당신이 날씬함을 유지하도록 도와줄 수 있어요.

_____

- - - - - - - - - - - -

_____

_____

ⓐ

---

straight
곧은, 똑바른

She has long straight hair.
그녀는 긴 생(곧은)머리예요.

_____

- - - - - - - - - - - -

_____

_____

ⓐ

---

control
조절하다, 통제

I should control my eating habits. (v)(n)

나는 식습관을 조절해야 해요.

_____
_____
_____

enough
충분한

I've had enough to eat. (pron)

저 충분히 먹었어요.

_____
_____
_____

lose
줄다, 잃다

I want to lose weight. (v)

나는 살을 빼고 싶어요.

_____
_____
_____

gain
얻다, 늘리다

Eating healthy can help you gain energy. (v)

건강하게 먹는 것은 에너지를 얻는 데 도움을 줄 수 있어요.

_____
_____
_____

consume
소모하다,
소비하다

Muscles consume energy all day long. (v)

근육은 하루 종일 에너지를 소모해요.

_____
_____
_____

Skill UP

A Choose and write the words.

thin	straight	lose

1 _____

줄다, 잃다

2 _____

마른, 얇은

3 _____

곧은, 똑바른

B Choose and write the words.

slim	gain	control	enough

1 조절하다, 통제 _____

2 얻다, 늘리다 _____

3 날씬한 _____

4 충분한 _____

C Connect and fill in the blanks.

1

I should control my eating habits.

나는 식습관을 _____야 해요.

2

I've had enough to eat.

저 _____ 먹었어요.

3

Muscles consume energy all day long.

근육은 하루 종일 에너지를 _____.

D Rearrange and write the sentences.

1 나는 살을 빼고 싶어요.

| weight | want | I | lose | to | . |

_____

- -

_____

2 그는 마르고 키가 커요.

| thin | is | tall | He | and | . |

_____

- -

_____

Day 04 Primitive Time

Check UP Read and check the words you don't know.

1차 복습

☐ thin	☐ enough
☐ slim	☐ lose
☐ straight	☐ gain
☐ control	☐ consume

2차 복습

☐ grandfather	☐ declare
☐ aunt	☐ formal

※ **망각 제로!** 1일 전 3일 전 학습한 단어를 복습해요.

Word Tip

thin 마른, 얇은   **slim** 날씬한   **straight** 곧은, 똑바른   **control** 조절하다, 통제

enough 충분한   **lose** 줄다, 잃다   **gain** 얻다, 늘리다   **consume** 소모하다, 소비하다

grandfather 할아버지   **aunt** 이모, 고모, 숙모   **declare** 선언하다   **formal** 격식을 차린, 정중한

How did primitive humans live?

Imagine how primitive humans survived.

They picked fruit in the forest.

POP Quiz Choose and check the right words.

**Kiara and her friends imagine
how primitive humans survived.**

키아라는 원시인들이 어떻게 ＿＿＿＿＿＿ 상상해 봐요.

- [ ] 사냥하다
- [ ] 살아남다

Primitive humans picked fruit in the forest.

원시인들은 ＿＿＿＿＿＿에서 과일을 땄어요.

- [ ] 동굴
- [ ] 숲

 **Listen & Say** Listen, say, and color.

Read & Write Write the **Basic Words** and **Jump Up Words**.

forest 숲	**There are bears in this forest.** ⓝ 이 숲에는 곰이 있어요. _____ _____ _____

cave 동굴	**There are bats in this cave.** ⓝ 이 동굴에는 박쥐가 있어요. _____ _____ _____

field 들판	**A bird is flying over the field.** ⓝ 새가 들판 위에서 날고 있어요. _____ _____ _____

hunt
사냥하다

Lions usually hunt at night. ⓥ

사자는 보통 밤에 사냥해요.

_____
- - - - - - - - - - - - - - -
_____

leaf
나뭇잎

A man is picking up a leaf. ⓝ

한 남자가 나뭇잎을 줍고 있어요.

_____
- - - - - - - - - - - - - - -
_____

primitive
원시의, 원시적인

Primitive people often lived in caves. ⓐ

원시인들은 주로 동굴에서 살았어요.

_____
- - - - - - - - - - - - - - -
_____

survive
살아남다

They needed to hunt to survive. ⓥ

그들은 살아남기 위해 사냥을 해야 했어요.

_____
- - - - - - - - - - - - - - -
_____

wild
야생, 야생의

They lived in the wild. ⓝ ⓐ

그들은 야생에 살았어요.

_____
- - - - - - - - - - - - - - -
_____

A Choose and write the words.

leaf	primitive	hunt

1

사냥하다

2

나뭇잎

3

원시의, 원시적인

B Choose and write the words.

wild	survive	field	forest

1 숲

----

2 살아남다

----

3 들판

----

4 야생, 야생의

C Unscramble and complete the sentences.

1

이 동굴에는 박쥐가 있어요.

`v c e a`

There are bats in this _____.

2

한 남자가 나뭇잎을 줍고 있어요.

`f l a e`

A man is picking up a _____.

3

이 숲에는 곰이 있어요.

`r e f o s t`

There are bears in this _____.

D Choose and complete the sentences.

Primitive   wild   hunt

1 사자는 보통 밤에 사냥해요.

Lions usually _____ at night.

2 원시인들은 주로 동굴에서 살았어요.

_____ people often lived in caves.

3 그들은 야생에 살았어요.

They lived in the _____.

Day 05 Comparisons

1차 복습

- ☐ forest
- ☐ cave
- ☐ field
- ☐ hunt
- ☐ leaf
- ☐ primitive
- ☐ survive
- ☐ wild

2차 복습

- ☐ mouse
- ☐ puppy
- ☐ feed
- ☐ responsible

※ **망각 제로!** 1일 전 3일 전 학습한 단어를 복습해요.

Word Tip

forest 숲	cave 동굴	field 들판	hunt 사냥하다
leaf 나뭇잎	primitive 원시의, 원시적인	survive 살아남다	wild 야생, 야생의
mouse 쥐	puppy 강아지	feed 먹이를 주다	responsible 책임감 있는

34

This is my twin sister.

Pop Quiz Choose and check the right words.

Rod's sisters are twins.

로드의 누나들은 _____ 예요.

☐ 단서
☐ 쌍둥이

Kamila and Lucia look exactly the same.

카밀라와 루시아는 정말 _____ 생겼어요.

☐ 같은
☐ 다른

 **Listen, say, and color.**

Read & Write Write the **Basic Words** and **Jump Up Words**.

---

easy
쉬운

I like English because it's easy.
나는 영어가 쉬워서 좋아요.

---

difficult
어려운

Science is more difficult than history.
과학은 역사보다 더 어려워요.

---

low
낮은

We got a low bowling score.
우리는 낮은 볼링 점수를 받았어요.

---

same
같은

I want the same one as hers.

나는 그녀와 같은 것을 갖고 싶어요.

_____

_____

different
다른

They look as different as night and day.

그들은 밤과 낮처럼 완전히 다르게 보여요.

_____

_____

confuse
혼동하다

People often confuse me with my twin sister.

사람들은 흔히 나와 내 쌍둥이 언니를 혼동해요.

_____

_____

clue
단서

Give me a clue about their differences.

차이점에 대한 단서를 주세요.

_____

_____

twin
쌍둥이

The twins look the same.

그 쌍둥이는 똑같이 생겼어요.

_____

_____

A Find, circle, and write the words.

1 낮은

o l o w s q n s

_____

2 쌍둥이

t w i n d f q a

_____

3 단서

q i e c l u e t

_____

4 혼동하다

c o n f u s e e

_____

B Cross out, unscramble, and write the words.

1 쉬운   y l s e a   _____

2 어려운   f f i d i t c u l w   _____

3 같은   s g a m e   _____

4 다른   t r e e f d i v f n   _____

C Connect and fill in the blanks.

1

Science is more difficult than history.

과학은 역사보다 더 _____요.

2

I want the same one as hers.

나는 그녀와 _____ 것을 갖고 싶어요.

3

Give me a clue about their differences.

차이점에 대한 _____를 주세요.

D Rearrange and write the sentences.

1 그 쌍둥이는 똑같이 생겼어요.

| The | look | the same | twins | . |

_____

_____

2 나는 영어가 쉬워서 좋아요.

| English | it's | I | easy | like | because | . |

_____

_____

WORD SEARCH

Find and circle the pictures.
Then write the words.

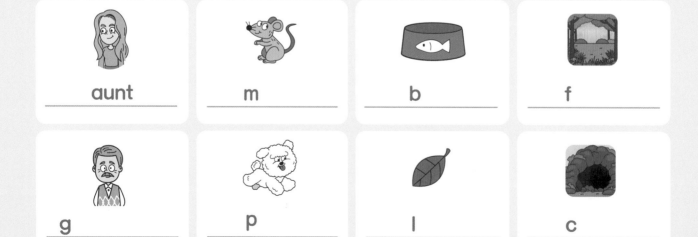

aunt	m_____	b_____	f_____
g_____	p_____	l_____	c_____

grandfather 할아버지	**aunt** 이모, 고모, 숙모	**uncle** 삼촌, 이모부, 고모부	**close** 가까운	**wedding** 결혼식
relative 친척	**declare** 선언하다	**formal** 격식을 차린, 정중한	**mouse** 쥐	**puppy** 강아지
bite 물다	**keep** 유지하다, 가지고 있다	**bowl** 그릇	**pet** 반려동물	**feed** 먹이를 주다
responsible 책임감 있는	**thin** 마른, 얇은	**slim** 날씬한	**straight** 곧은, 똑바른	**control** 조절하다, 통제
enough 충분한	**lose** 줄다, 잃다	**gain** 얻다, 늘리다	**consume** 소모하다, 소비하다	**forest** 숲
cave 동굴	**field** 들판	**hunt** 사냥하다	**leaf** 나뭇잎	**primitive** 원시의, 원시적인
survive 살아남다	**wild** 야생, 야생의	**easy** 쉬운	**difficult** 어려운	**low** 낮은
same 같은	**different** 다른	**confuse** 혼동하다	**clue** 단서	**twin** 쌍둥이

Review TEST

❶ grandfather		㉑ 결혼식	
❷ aunt		㉒ 친척	
❸ uncle		㉓ 선언하다	
❹ formal		㉔ 가까운	
❺ mouse		㉕ 그릇	
❻ puppy		㉖ 반려동물	
❼ bite		㉗ 먹이를 주다	
❽ keep		㉘ 책임감 있는	
❾ thin		㉙ 충분한	
❿ consume		㉚ 줄다, 잃다	
⓫ straight		㉛ 얻다, 늘리다	
⓬ control		㉜ 날씬한	
⓭ forest		㉝ 나뭇잎	
⓮ primitive		㉞ 동굴	
⓯ field		㉟ 살아남다	
⓰ hunt		㊱ 야생, 야생의	
⓱ easy		㊲ 다른	
⓲ difficult		㊳ 혼동하다	
⓳ low		㊴ 단서	
⓴ same		㊵ 쌍둥이	

Part 2

FINISH

START

Day 06 Earth & Space

Check Up Read and check the words you don't know.

1차 복습

- [ ] easy
- [ ] difficult
- [ ] low
- [ ] same
- [ ] different
- [ ] confuse
- [ ] clue
- [ ] twin

2차 복습

- [ ] thin
- [ ] slim
- [ ] gain
- [ ] consume

※ 망각 제로! 1일 전 3일 전 학습한 단어를 복습해요.

 **Word Tip**

easy 쉬운	**difficult** 어려운	**low** 낮은	**same** 같은
different 다른	**confuse** 혼동하다	**clue** 단서	**twin** 쌍둥이
thin 마른, 얇은	**slim** 날씬한	**gain** 얻다, 늘리다	**consume** 소모하다, 소비하다

What is the pale blue dot?

It's Earth, the planet we live on.

그것은 우리가 살고 있는 행성, _____ 예요.

☐ 지구

☐ 우주

About 71% of Earth's surface is ocean water.

지구 _____의 약 71%가 바닷물이예요.

☐ 표면

☐ 행성

Catch Up

Read & Write   Write the **Basic Words** and **Jump Up Words**.

---

space
우주

The astronaut is exploring space.

우주 비행사는 우주를 탐험하고 있어요.

_____

_____

_____

Earth
지구

We should save Earth.

우리는 지구를 구해야 해요.

_____

_____

_____

---

ocean
바다, 대양

The Pacific Ocean is the largest ocean on Earth.

태평양은 지구에서 가장 큰 바다예요.

_____

_____

_____

ground
땅

The ground was wet and muddy. (n)

땅은 축축하고, 진흙투성이였어요.

---

around
~ 주위에, 주변에

The children gathered around the telescope. (prep)

아이들은 망원경 주위에 모였어요.

---

planet
행성

Mercury is the smallest planet. (n)

수성은 가장 작은 행성이에요.

---

dot
점

My house looks like a dot on the map. (n)

내 집은 지도에서 점처럼 보여요.

---

surface
표면

Water covers most of Earth's surface. (n)

물은 지구 표면 대부분을 덮고 있어요.

A Choose and write the words.

around	ground	ocean

1

바다, 대양

2

~ 주위에, 주변에

3

땅

B Choose and write the words.

space	dot	surface	planet

1 표면

2 점

3 행성

4 우주

C Connect and fill in the blanks.

1

The astrorant is exploring space.

우주 비행사는 _____ 를 탐험하고 있어요.

2

My house looks like a dot on the map.

내 집은 지도에서 _____ 처럼 보여요.

3

Water covers most of Earth's surface.

물은 지구 _____ 대부분을 덮고 있어요.

D Rearrange and write the sentences.

1 우리는 지구를 구해야 해요.

| save | We | Earth | should | . |

---

2 땅은 축축하고, 진흙투성이였어요.

| was | and | wet | muddy | The | ground | . |

Day 07 Activities

Check Up Read and check the words you don't know.

1차 복습

- [ ] space
- [ ] Earth
- [ ] ocean
- [ ] ground
- [ ] around
- [ ] planet
- [ ] dot
- [ ] surface

2차 복습

- [ ] forest
- [ ] cave
- [ ] survive
- [ ] wild

3차 복습

- [ ] uncle
- [ ] close
- [ ] wedding
- [ ] relative

※망각 제로! 1일 전 3일 전 7일 전 학습한 단어를 복습해요.

space 우주	Earth 지구	ocean 바다, 대양	ground 땅
around ~ 주위에, 주변에	planet 행성	dot 점	surface 표면
forest 숲	cave 동굴	survive 살아남다	wild 야생, 야생의
uncle 삼촌, 이모부, 고모부	close 가까운	wedding 결혼식	relative 친척

Rod has a new hobby.

Pop Quiz Choose and check the right words.

Solving jigsaw puzzles is Rod's new hobby.

퍼즐을 푸는 것은 로드의 새로운 _____ 예요.

- [ ] 퍼즐
- [ ] 취미

Solving jigsaw puzzles is good for the brain and memory.

퍼즐을 푸는 것은 _____ 와 기억력에 좋아요.

- [ ] 두뇌, 뇌
- [ ] 주문

Write the Basic Words and Jump Up Words.

| puzzle
퍼즐,
수수께끼 | He put the puzzle together. (n)
그는 퍼즐을 맞추었어요. |

| hobby
취미 | One of my hobbies is taking pictures. (n)
내 취미 중의 하나는 사진 찍기예요. |

| memory
기억(력) | Memory is the key point of the game. (n)
기억력은 그 게임의 핵심이에요. |

brain
두뇌, 뇌

Solving puzzles is
a good brain activity.

퍼즐을 푸는 것은 좋은 두뇌 활동이에요.

_____
_____
_____

side
(좌우 절반 중 한)
쪽

Fold the paper to the left side.

종이를 왼쪽으로 접으세요.

_____
_____
_____

available
구할 수 있는

Tickets are available
from the box office.

입장권은 매표소에서 구할 수 있어요.

_____
_____
_____

order
주문하다, 주문

Did you order your tickets online?

온라인으로 입장권을 주문하셨나요?

_____
_____
_____

relieve
없애 주다,
완화하다

It's a very good way
to relieve stress.

그건 스트레스 없애는 데 아주 좋은 방법이에요.

_____
_____
_____

53

A Choose and write the words.

side	brain	memory

①

_____

_ _ _ _ _ _ _ _ _ _ _

_____

두뇌, 뇌

②

_____

_ _ _ _ _ _ _ _ _ _ _

_____

(좌우 절반 중 한) 쪽

③

_____

_ _ _ _ _ _ _ _ _ _ _

_____

기억(력)

B Choose and write the words.

puzzle	order	relieve	hobby

① 퍼즐, 수수께끼

② 취미

③ 주문하다, 주문

④ 없애 주다, 완화하다

C Unscramble and complete the sentences.

1
그는 퍼즐을 맞추었어요.

p z l u e z

He put the _____ together.

2
입장권은 매표소에서 구할 수 있어요.

l a a v i l a b e

Tickets are _____ from the box office.

3
온라인으로 입장권을 주문하셨나요?

e r r o d

Did you _____ your tickets online?

D Choose and complete the sentences.

Memory   relieve   hobbies

1 기억력은 그 게임의 핵심이에요.

_____ is the key point of the game.

2 내 취미 중의 하나는 사진 찍기예요.

One of my _____ is taking pictures.

3 그건 스트레스 없애는 데 아주 좋은 방법이에요.

It's a very good way to _____ stress.

Day 08 Culture & Rituals

Check Up Read and check the words you don't know.

1차 복습

- [ ] puzzle
- [ ] hobby
- [ ] memory
- [ ] brain
- [ ] side
- [ ] available
- [ ] order
- [ ] relieve

2차 복습

- [ ] easy
- [ ] difficult
- [ ] clue
- [ ] twin

3차 복습

- [ ] bite
- [ ] keep
- [ ] bowl
- [ ] pet

※ **망각 제로!** 1일 전 3일 전 7일 전 학습한 단어를 복습해요.

Word Tip

puzzle 퍼즐, 수수께끼	**hobby** 취미	**memory** 기억(력)	**brain** 두뇌, 뇌
side (좌우 절반 중 한) 쪽	**available** 구할 수 있는	**order** 주문하다, 주문	**relieve** 없애 주다, 완화하다
easy 쉬운	**difficult** 어려운	**clue** 단서	**twin** 쌍둥이
bite 물다	**keep** 유지하다, 가지고 있다	**bowl** 그릇	**pet** 반려동물

56

Do you believe in an afterlife?

POP QUIZ Choose and check the right words.

People are burying the coffin.

사람들이 관을 _____ 있어요.

- [ ] 교회
- [ ] 묻다

Do you believe in life after death?

너희들은 사후 세계를 _____?

- [ ] 무덤
- [ ] 믿다

57

Listen, say, and color.

Write the Basic Words and Jump Up Words.

church 교회	My parents go to church every Sunday. 우리 부모님은 매주 일요일에 교회에 가요.	n

death 죽음	His death was very sudden. 그의 죽음은 갑작스러웠어요.	n

one 하나, 하나의	Everyone lights one candle. 모두가 촛불을 하나씩 밝혀요.	num det

believe
믿다

They believe drums are important for their ritual.

그들은 드럼이 그들의 의식에 중요하다고 믿어요.

ⓥ

---

culture
문화

I'm very proud of my traditional culture.

나는 전통문화가 매우 자랑스러워요.

ⓝ

---

funeral
장례식

Hundreds of people attended the funeral.

수백 명의 사람들이 그 장례식에 참석했어요.

ⓝ

---

grave
산소, 무덤

We visited Grandfather's grave.

우리는 할아버지의 산소에 방문했어요.

ⓝ

---

bury
묻다,
매장하다

We bury the dead in cemeteries.

우리는 죽은 사람을 묘지에 묻어요.

ⓥ

A Find, circle, and write the words.

1 교회

churchiik

_____

2 죽음

usideath

_____

3 믿다

abelieve

_____

4 산소, 무덤

cgravere

_____

B Cross out, unscramble, and write the words.

1 하나, 하나의 peon _____

2 장례식 fknurela _____

3 문화 utculrew _____

4 묻다, 매장하다 yumbr _____

C Connect and fill in the blanks.

1

Everyone lights one candle.

모두가 촛불을 _____씩 밝혀요.

2

I'm very proud of my traditional culture.

나는 전통_____가 매우 자랑스러워요.

3

We bury the dead in cemeteries.

우리는 죽은 사람을 묘지에 _____.

D Rearrange and write the sentences.

1 그의 죽음은 갑작스러웠어요.

| sudden | was | very | death | His | . |

_____

- -

_____

2 우리는 할아버지의 산소에 방문했어요.

| grave | We | Grandfather's | visited | . |

_____

- -

_____

Day 09 School Life

Check Up Read and check the words you don't know.

1차 복습

- [ ] church
- [ ] death
- [ ] one
- [ ] believe
- [ ] culture
- [ ] funeral
- [ ] grave
- [ ] bury

2차 복습

- [ ] space
- [ ] Earth
- [ ] dot
- [ ] surface

3차 복습

- [ ] straight
- [ ] control
- [ ] enough
- [ ] lose

※ **망각 제로!** 1일 전 3일 전 7일 전 학습한 단어를 복습해요.

Word Tip

church 교회   death 죽음   one 하나, 하나의   believe 믿다
culture 문화   funeral 장례식   grave 산소, 무덤   bury 묻다, 매장하다
space 우주   Earth 지구   dot 점   surface 표면
straight 곧은, 똑바른   control 조절하다, 통제   enough 충분한   lose 줄다, 잃다

I hate exams!

Pop Quiz Choose and check the right words.

Kiara failed the exam.

키아라는 _____을 망쳤어요.

☐ 점수

☐ 시험

Sally hates exams.

샐리는 시험을 _____.

☐ 몹시 싫어하다

☐ (시험에) 떨어지다

Catch Up

 **Listen & Say** Listen, say, and color.

Read & Write Write the **Basic Words** and **Jump Up Words**.

exam 시험	**How did you do on your exams?** ⓝ 시험 잘 봤어요? _____ _____

hate 몹시 싫어하다	**I hate to see you fight.** ⓥ 나는 당신이 싸우는 것 보기 싫어요. _____ _____

fail (시험에) 떨어지다	**He failed the exam by just one point.** ⓥ 그는 딱 1점이 모자라서 시험에서 떨어졌어요. _____ _____ _____ 

64

score
점수

Your test scores were very impressive.

당신의 시험 점수가 매우 인상적이었어요.

_____
_____
_____

fact
사실

We learn many facts at school.

우리는 학교에서 많은 사실을 배워요.

_____
_____
_____

correct
정확한, 옳은

That is the correct answer.

저것은 정확한 답이에요.

_____
_____
_____

mental
정신의, 마음의

Stress is harmful to your mental health.

스트레스는 정신 건강에 해로워요.

_____
_____
_____

grade
학년, 성적

I'm in the sixth grade.

나는 6학년이에요.

_____
_____
_____

A Choose and write the words.

mental	fail	score

1

_____

(시험에) 떨어지다

2

_____

정신의, 마음의

3

_____

점수

B Choose and write the words.

exam	correct	score	fact

1 시험

_____ _____

2 점수

_____ _____

3 사실

_____ _____

4 정확한, 옳은

_____ _____

C Connect and fill in the blanks.

1.

How did you do on your exams?

_____ 잘 봤어요?

2.

I hate to see you fight.

나는 당신이 싸우는 것 보기 _____.

3.

We learn many facts at school.

우리는 학교에서 많은 _____ 을 배워요.

D Rearrange and write the sentences.

1. 저것은 정확한 답이에요.

| correct | That | answer | is | the | . |

_____

_____

_____

2. 나는 6학년이에요.

| in | I'm | sixth | the | grade | . |

_____

_____

_____

Day 10 Trip

1차 복습

- [ ] exam
- [ ] hate
- [ ] fail
- [ ] score

- [ ] fact
- [ ] correct
- [ ] mental
- [ ] grade

2차 복습

- [ ] puzzle
- [ ] hobby

- [ ] order
- [ ] relieve

3차 복습

- [ ] field
- [ ] hunt

- [ ] leaf
- [ ] primitive

※ 망각 제로! 1일 전 3일 전 7일 전 학습한 단어를 복습해요.

Word Tip

exam 시험	hate 몹시 싫어하다	fail (시험에) 떨어지다	score 점수
fact 사실	correct 정확한, 옳은	mental 정신의, 마음의	grade 학년, 성적
puzzle 퍼즐, 수수께끼	hobby 취미	order 주문하다, 주문	relieve 없애 주다, 완화하다
field 들판	hunt 사냥하다	leaf 나뭇잎	primitive 원시의, 원시적인

Have you ever traveled alone?

POP Quiz Choose and check the right words.

Sally took a day trip alone.

샐리는 혼자 당일치기 _____을 했어요.

☐ 여행

☐ 풍경

Sally went to the countryside.

샐리는 _____에 갔어요.

☐ 시골 지역

☐ 혼자

Catch Up

 **Listen, say, and color.**

 Write the Basic Words and Jump Up Words.

trip 여행	**We went on a trip to France.** ⓝ 우리는 프랑스로 여행을 갔어요. _____ - - - - - - - - - - - - - - - - _____

street 길, 거리	**I used my smartphone to find the street.** ⓝ 나는 길을 찾기 위해 스마트폰을 사용했어요. _____ - - - - - - - - - - - - - - - - _____

explore 탐험하다	**We explored the jungle.** ⓥ 우리는 정글을 탐험했어요. _____ - - - - - - - - - - - - - - - - _____

70

alone
혼자

Traveling alone is a good experience. *(a)*

혼자 여행하는 것은 좋은 경험이에요.

countryside
시골 지역

I like to go to the countryside. *(n)*

나는 시골에 가는 것을 좋아해요.

challenge
도전, 도전하다

This is a new challenge for me. *(n)(v)*

이건 내게 새로운 도전이에요.

landscape
풍경

The landscape is very beautiful. *(n)*

풍경이 매우 아름다워요.

route
경로, 길

GPS finds the shortest route. *(n)*

GPS가 가장 짧은 경로를 찾아요.

A Choose and write the words.

| landscape | street | explore |

1

_____
_____
_____

탐험하다

2

_____
_____
_____

풍경

3

_____
_____
_____

길, 거리

B Choose and write the words.

| alone | countryside | trip | route |

1 경로, 길

_____
_____
_____

_____
_____
_____

2 혼자

_____
_____
_____

_____
_____
_____

3 시골 지역

_____
_____
_____

_____
_____
_____

4 여행

_____
_____
_____

_____
_____
_____

C Unscramble and complete the sentences.

1
우리는 프랑스로 여행을 갔어요.

i p r t

We went on a _____ to France.

2
GPS가 가장 짧은 경로를 찾아요.

r e o u t

GPS finds the shortest _____.

3
이건 내게 새로운 도전이에요.

g e c h l l a n e

This is a new _____ for me.

D Choose and complete the sentences.

explored   street   landscape

1 우리는 정글을 탐험했어요.

We _____ the jungle.

2 풍경이 매우 아름다워요.

The _____ is very beautiful.

3 나는 길을 찾기 위해 스마트폰을 사용했어요.

I used my smartphone to find the _____.

WORD SEARCH Find, circle, and write the words.

Words go in 2 directions → ↓

s	f	w	m	e	m	o	r	y	e
p	a	y	n	n	j	u	z	u	x
a	i	s	t	r	e	e	t	j	a
c	l	x	c	h	u	r	c	h	m
e	x	g	u	t	j	c	f	m	z
e	t	m	l	p	l	a	n	e	t
k	r	l	t	c	f	o	m	m	k
o	i	h	u	c	k	m	r	o	y
b	p	e	r	v	c	t	r	a	m
s	d	y	e	s	i	d	e	y	p

Word Bank

side   fail
exam   trip
space   planet
memory   street
church   culture

space

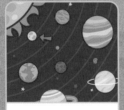

space 우주	Earth 지구	ocean 바다, 대양	ground 땅	around ~ 주위에, 주변에
planet 행성	dot 점	surface 표면	puzzle 퍼즐, 수수께끼	hobby 취미
memory 기억(력)	brain 두뇌, 뇌	side (좌우 절반 중 한) 쪽	available 구할 수 있는	order 주문하다, 주문
relieve 없애 주다, 완화하다	church 교회	death 죽음	one 하나, 하나의	believe 믿다
culture 문화	funeral 장례식	grave 산소, 무덤	bury 묻다, 매장하다	exam 시험
hate 몹시 싫어하다	fail (시험에) 떨어지다	score 점수	fact 사실	correct 정확한, 옳은
mental 정신의, 마음의	grade 학년, 성적	trip 여행	street 길, 거리	explore 탐험하다
alone 혼자	countryside 시골 지역	challenge 도전, 도전하다	landscape 풍경	route 경로, 길

Day
06~10

Review TEST

맞힌 개수 : [ ] /40

① space		㉑ ~ 주위에, 주변에	
② Earth		㉒ 행성	
③ ocean		㉓ 점	
④ ground		㉔ 표면	
⑤ side		㉕ 퍼즐, 수수께끼	
⑥ relieve		㉖ 구할 수 있는	
⑦ memory		㉗ 주문하다, 주문	
⑧ brain		㉘ 두뇌, 뇌	
⑨ church		㉙ 문화	
⑩ death		㉚ 장례식	
⑪ one		㉛ 산소, 무덤	
⑫ believe		㉜ 묻다, 매장하다	
⑬ exam		㉝ 사실	
⑭ hate		㉞ 정확한, 옳은	
⑮ fail		㉟ 정신의, 마음의	
⑯ score		㊱ 학년, 성적	
⑰ trip		㊲ 시골 지역	
⑱ street		㊳ 도전, 도전하다	
⑲ explore		㊴ 풍경	
⑳ alone		㊵ 경로, 길	

Part 3

FINISH

START

Day 11 Events

Check Up Read and check the words you don't know.

☐ trip   ☐ countryside
☐ street   ☐ challenge
☐ explore   ☐ landscape
☐ alone   ☐ route

☐ church   ☐ grave
☐ death   ☐ bury

☐ low   ☐ different
☐ same   ☐ confuse

※망각 제로! 1일 전 3일 전 7일 전 학습한 단어를 복습해요.

Word Tip

trip 여행
countryside 시골 지역
church 교회
low 낮은

street 길, 거리
challenge 도전, 도전하다
death 죽음
same 같은

explore 탐험하다
landscape 풍경
grave 산소, 무덤
different 다른

alone 혼자
route 경로, 길
bury 묻다, 매장하다
confuse 혼동하다

78

What did you do last weekend?

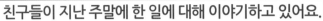

Pop Quiz Choose and check the right words.

Sally watched a comedy movie.
샐리는 _____ 영화를 봤어요.

☐ 가게

☐ 코미디

Rod went to a special restaurant.
로드는 특별한 _____ 에 갔어요.

☐ 식당

☐ 극장

 **Listen, say, and color.**

 Write the Basic Words and Jump Up Words.

restaurant 식당	**We went to an Italian restaurant.** ⁿ 우리는 이탈리안 식당에 갔어요. _____
shop 가게	**The shop sells fresh local produce.** ⁿ 그 가게는 신선한 지역 농산물을 팔아요. _____
after (시간상으로) 뒤에, 후에	**We'll leave after dinner.** prep conj 우리는 저녁 식사 이후 떠날 거예요. _____

before
(시간상으로)
전에, 앞에

Wash your hands before eating. prep conj

먹기 전에 손을 씻으세요.

_____
_____
_____

comedy
코미디, 희극

I like to watch comedies. n

나는 코미디 보는 것을 좋아해요.

_____
_____
_____

theater
극장

He works at a movie theater. n

그는 영화관에서 일해요.

_____
_____
_____

terrible
끔찍한, 형편없는

It was a terrible accident. a

그것은 끔찍한 사고였어요.

_____
_____
_____

special
특별한

I have special plans for this weekend. a

나는 이번 주말에 특별한 계획이 있어요.

_____
_____
_____

A Find, circle, and write the words.

1 가게
olshopie
_____

2 (시간상으로)
뒤에, 후에
trafterc
_____

3 (시간상으로)
전에, 앞에
aubefore
_____

4 코미디, 희극
comedyct
_____

B Cross out, unscramble, and write the words.

1 식당
eaatruntsrl
_____

2 극장
nhttreae
_____

3 끔찍한, 형편없는
rritqbele
_____

4 특별한
ylipscea
_____

C Connect and fill in the blanks.

1

We went to an Italian restaurant.

우리는 이탈리안 _____ 에 갔어요.

2

I like to watch comedies.

나는 _____ 보는 것을 좋아해요.

3

I have special plans
for this weekend.

나는 이번 주말에 _____ 계획이 있어요.

D Rearrange and write the sentences.

1 그것은 끔찍한 사고였어요.

| a | was | It | accident | terrible | . |

2 우리는 저녁 식사 이후 떠날 거예요.

| leave | We'll | dinner | after | . |

Day 12 Entertainment

Check Up Read and check the words you don't know.

1차 복습

- [ ] restaurant
- [ ] shop
- [ ] after
- [ ] before
- [ ] comedy
- [ ] theater
- [ ] terrible
- [ ] special

2차 복습

- [ ] exam
- [ ] hate
- [ ] mental
- [ ] grade

3차 복습

- [ ] ocean
- [ ] ground
- [ ] around
- [ ] planet

※ 망각 제로! 1일 전 3일 전 7일 전 학습한 단어를 복습해요.

Word Tip

restaurant 식당	**shop** 가게	**after** (시간상으로) 뒤에, 후에	**before** (시간상으로) 전에, 앞에
comedy 코미디, 희극	**theater** 극장	**terrible** 끔찍한, 형편없는	**special** 특별한
exam 시험	**hate** 몹시 싫어하다	**mental** 정신의, 마음의	**grade** 학년, 성적
ocean 바다, 대양	**ground** 땅	**around** ~ 주위에, 주변에	**planet** 행성

What are the best concert seats?

Pop Quiz Choose and check the right words.

Kiara's favorite musician is having a concert next month.

키아라가 좋아하는 음악가가 다음 달에 _____를 해요.

☐ 콘서트
☐ 영화관

You can hear the best sound in the middle of the hall.

가장 좋은 소리를 들을 수 있는 자리는 홀의 _____이에요.

☐ 중앙, 가운데의
☐ 앞쪽의, 앞면

Catch Up

Listen, say, and color.

Write the Basic Words and Jump Up Words.

---

cinema
영화관

Why don't we go to the cinema tonight?

오늘 밤 영화관에 가지 않을래요?

_____
_____
_____

---

concert
콘서트, 연주회

Her first concert is a great success.

그녀의 첫 콘서트는 대성공이었어요.

_____
_____
_____

---

sound
소리, 연주

I like their sound.

나는 그들의 연주가 좋아요.

_____
_____
_____

front
앞쪽의, 앞면

I got a seat in the front row. ⓐⓝ

나는 앞쪽 줄의 좌석을 구했어요.

---

middle
중앙, 가운데의

He is standing in the middle of the stage. ⓝⓐ

그는 무대 중앙에 서 있어요.

---

screen
화면

I can see him on the screen. ⓝ

그를 화면에서 볼 수 있어요.

---

row
(극장 등의 좌석)
줄

I was sitting in the second row. ⓝ

나는 두 번째 줄에 앉아 있었어요.

---

depend
~에 달려 있다,
좌우되다

Does the musical depend on the cast? ⓥ

그 뮤지컬은 출연자에 따라 달라지나요?

A Choose and write the words.

middle	sound	concert

1 _____

콘서트, 연주회

2 _____

소리, 연주

3 _____

중앙, 가운데의

B Choose and write the words.

cinema	row	depend	front

1 영화관 _____

2 앞쪽의, 앞면 _____

3 (극장 등의 좌석) 줄 _____

4 ~에 달려 있다, 좌우되다 _____

C Connect and fill in the blanks.

1

I can see him on the screen.

그를 _____에서 볼 수 있어요.

2

I was sitting in the second row.

나는 두 번째 _____에 앉아 있었어요.

3

Why don't we go to the cinema tonight?

오늘 밤 _____에 가지 않을래요?

D Rearrange and write the sentences.

1 나는 그들의 연주가 좋아요.

| sound | like | their | I | . |

_____

_____

_____

2 그녀의 첫 콘서트는 대성공이었어요.

| sucess | first | concert | is | a | great | Her | . |

_____

_____

_____

Day 13 Shopping

Check Up Read and check the words you don't know.

1차 복습

- ☐ cinema
- ☐ concert
- ☐ sound
- ☐ front

- ☐ middle
- ☐ screen
- ☐ row
- ☐ depend

2차 복습

- ☐ trip
- ☐ street

- ☐ landscape
- ☐ route

3차 복습

- ☐ memory
- ☐ brain

- ☐ side
- ☐ available

※ 망각 제로! 1일 전 3일 전 7일 전 학습한 단어를 복습해요.

Word Tip

cinema 영화관	concert 콘서트, 연주회	sound 소리, 연주	front 앞쪽의, 앞면
middle 중앙, 가운데의	screen 화면	row (극장 등의 좌석) 줄	depend ~에 달려 있다, 좌우되다
trip 여행	street 길, 거리	landscape 풍경	route 경로, 길
memory 기억(력)	brain 두뇌, 뇌	side (좌우 절반 중 한) 쪽	available 구할 수 있는

90

Let's have a garage sale!

데니스의 가족이 차고에서 중고 물품을 판매해요.
Dennis's family is selling their used goods in a garage sale.

Pop Quiz Choose and check the right words.

Dennis's family is selling their used goods in a garage sale.

데니스의 가족이 차고에서 중고 물품을 _____.

☐ 팔다
☐ 확인하다

A woman checks out a hat in a mirror.

한 여성이 _____로 모자를 확인해요.

☐ 거울
☐ 현금

 **Listen, say, and color.**

Read & Write Write the **Basic Words** and **Jump Up Words**.

sell 팔다	**The store sells some organic products.** v 그 가게는 유기농 제품을 팔아요. _____ ------------------ _____

customer 손님, 고객	**This clothing store has many regular customers.** n 이 옷 가게는 단골 손님이 많아요. _____ ------------------ _____

cash 현금, 돈	**How much cash do you have?** n 현금을 얼마나 가지고 계시나요? _____ ------------------

check
확인하다

Check your shopping list. (v)

쇼핑 목록을 확인해 보세요.

mirror
거울

My sister is looking in the mirror. (n)

내 여동생은 거울을 들여다보고 있어요.

price
가격

The store marked their prices down. (n)

그 가게는 가격을 낮췄어요.

slide
미끄럼틀,
미끄러지다

The toy store has a big slide. (n)(v)

장난감 가게에는 큰 미끄럼틀이 있어요.

goods
상품

There are a lot of goods in the store. (n)

그 가게에는 많은 상품이 있어요.

A Choose and write the words.

mirror	price	customer

1

_____
_____
_____

손님, 고객

2

_____
_____
_____

거울

3

_____
_____
_____

가격

B Choose and write the words.

sell	goods	check	cash

1 팔다

2 현금, 돈

3 확인하다

4 상품

C Unscramble and complete the sentences.

1

그 가게는 유기농 제품을 팔아요.

l l s e s

The store _____ some organic products.

2

현금을 얼마나 가지고 계시나요?

a h c s

How much _____ do you have?

3

쇼핑 목록을 확인해 보세요.

c e k h C

_____ your shopping list.

D Choose and complete the sentences.

slide   mirror   goods

1 내 여동생은 기울을 들여다보고 있어요.

My sister is looking in the _____.

2 그 가게에는 많은 상품이 있어요.

There are a lot of _____ in the store.

3 장난감 가게에는 큰 미끄럼틀이 있어요.

The toy store has a big _____.

Day 14 Geography & Architecture

Check Up Read and check the words you don't know.

1차 복습

- [ ] sell
- [ ] customer
- [ ] cash
- [ ] check
- [ ] mirror
- [ ] price
- [ ] slide
- [ ] goods

2차 복습

- [ ] restaurant
- [ ] shop
- [ ] terrible
- [ ] special

3차 복습

- [ ] one
- [ ] believe
- [ ] culture
- [ ] funeral

※ 망각 제로! 1일 전 3일 전 7일 전 학습한 단어를 복습해요.

Word Tip

sell 팔다	customer 손님, 고객	cash 현금, 돈	check 확인하다
mirror 거울	price 가격	slide 미끄럼틀, 미끄러지다	goods 상품
restaurant 식당	shop 가게	terrible 끔찍한, 형편없는	special 특별한
one 하나, 하나의	believe 믿다	culture 문화	funeral 장례식

Have you been to the UK?

London is the capital of the UK.

런던은 영국의 _____ 예요.

- [ ] 수도
- [ ] 궁전

Tower Bridge is a famous structure in London.

타워 브리지는 런던의 유명한 _____ 이에요.

- [ ] 구조물
- [ ] 땅

Read & Write Write the **Basic Words** and **Jump Up Words**.

| live | **I live in London.** |
| 살다 | 나는 런던에 살아요. |

| land | **The land is located in the south.** |
| 땅 | 그 땅은 남쪽에 위치해 있어요. |

| bridge | **A stone bridge crosses the stream.** |
| 다리 | 돌다리가 시내를 가로질러요. |

98

palace
궁전

He wants to visit palaces in Seoul. ⓝ

그는 서울에 있는 궁전들을 방문하고 싶어 해요.

---

capital
수도

London is the capital of the UK. ⓝ

런던은 영국의 수도예요.

---

address
주소,
주소를 쓰다

What is this building's address? ⓝ ⓥ

이 건물의 주소는 무엇인가요?

---

structure
구조, 구조물

The structure of this building is complicated. ⓝ

이 건물은 구조가 복잡해요.

---

resource
자원

We should not waste resources such as water. ⓝ

우리는 물과 같은 자원을 낭비해서는 안 돼요.

Skill UP

A Find, circle, and write the words.

1 살다
o l e l i v e n

2 궁전
l a p a l a c e n

3 수도
n c a p i t a l

4 주소,
주소를 쓰다
a d d r e s s s

B Cross out, unscramble, and write the words.

1 다리
d e b r i g o

2 땅
a l c n d

3 구조,
구조물
s t r e u r t c k u

4 자원
r h r e u s e c o

C Connect and fill in the blanks.

1.
The land is located in the south.

그 _____은 남쪽에 위치해 있어요.

2.
A stone bridge crosses the stream.

돌_____가 시내를 가로질러요.

3.
The structure of this building is complicated.

이 건물은 _____가 복잡해요.

D Rearrange and write the sentences.

1 나는 런던에 살아요.

| in | I | London | live | . |

_____

_____

_____

2 이 건물의 주소는 무엇인가요?

| building's | What | address | is | this | ? |

_____

_____

_____

Day 15 Rules & Policies

Check Up Read and check the words you don't know.

1차 복습

- [ ] live
- [ ] land
- [ ] bridge
- [ ] palace
- [ ] capital
- [ ] address
- [ ] structure
- [ ] resource

2차 복습

- [ ] cinema
- [ ] concert
- [ ] row
- [ ] depend

3차 복습

- [ ] fail
- [ ] score
- [ ] fact
- [ ] correct

※ 망각 제로! 1일 전 3일 전 7일 전 학습한 단어를 복습해요.

Word Tip

live 살다	land 땅	bridge 다리	palace 궁전
capital 수도	address 주소, 주소를 쓰다	structure 구조, 구조물	resource 자원
cinema 영화관	concert 콘서트, 연주회	row (극장 등의 좌석) 줄	depend ~에 달려 있다, 좌우되다
fail (시험에) 떨어지다	score 점수	fact 사실	correct 정확한, 옳은

Let's order some pizza!

Pop Quiz Choose and check the right words.

The pizza has arrived.

피자가 _____.

☐ 도착하다

☐ 들어가다

Pizza used to be free if it wasn't delivered in 30 minutes.

피자가 30분 안에 배달되지 않으면 _____요.

☐ 사실인

☐ 무료의

Catch Up

 **Listen, say, and color.**

Read & Write Write the **Basic Words** and **Jump Up Words**.

---

enter
들어가다

You may not enter this area. ⓥ

이 영역에는 들어갈 수 없어요.

_____

_____

---

arrive
도착하다

I should arrive at home before 8 o'clock. ⓥ

저는 8시 전에 집에 도착해야 해요.

_____

_____

---

free
무료의,
자유로운

Admission is free today. ⓐ

오늘은 입장료가 무료예요.

_____

_____

true
사실인, 진짜의

It is true that policies can be changed.

정책이 변경될 수 있는 것은 사실이에요.

_____
_____
_____

design
디자인하다, 설계하다

He designs all his own clothes.

그는 모든 옷을 직접 디자인해요.

_____
_____
_____

deliver
배달하다

The food is free if we deliver it late.

우리가 늦게 배달하면 음식은 무료예요.

_____
_____
_____

policy
정책, 방침

The new policy was adopted.

새로운 정책이 채택되었어요.

_____
_____
_____

limit
제한하다, 제한, 한도

My mom limits my screen time.

우리 엄마는 내 스크린 타임을 제한해요.

_____
_____
_____

A Choose and write the words.

free	arrive	design

1
디자인하다, 설계하다

2
도착하다

3
무료의, 자유로운

B Choose and write the words.

limit	true	policy	enter

1 들어가다

2 정책, 방침

3 사실인, 진짜의

4 제한하다, 제한, 한도

C Connect and fill in the blanks.

① **The food is free if we deliver it late.**

우리가 늦게 _____ 음식은 무료예요.

② **It is true that policies can be changed.**

정책이 변경될 수 있는 것은 _____ 이에요.

③ **My mom limits my screen time.**

우리 엄마는 내 스크린 타임을 _____.

D Rearrange and write the sentences.

① 오늘은 입장료가 무료예요.

| free | Admission | today | is | . |

_____

_____

② 새로운 정책이 채택되었어요.

| was | The | adopted | new | policy | . |

_____

_____

WORD PUZZLE Complete the word puzzle.

WORD BANK

live ★ sell
land ★ cash
enter ★ comedy
sound ★ shop
cinema ★ free

108

 **restaurant** 식당	**shop** 가게	**after** (시간상으로) 뒤에, 후에	**before** (시간상으로) 전에, 앞에	**comedy** 코미디, 희극
theater 극장	**terrible** 끔찍한, 형편없는	**special** 특별한	**cinema** 영화관	**concert** 콘서트, 연주회
sound 소리, 연주	**front** 앞쪽의, 앞면	**middle** 중앙, 가운데의	**screen** 화면	**row** (극장 등의 좌석) 줄
depend ~에 달려 있다, 좌우되다	**sell** 팔다	**customer** 손님, 고객	**cash** 현금, 돈	**check** 확인하다
mirror 거울	**price** 가격	**slide** 미끄럼틀, 미끄러지다	**goods** 상품	**live** 살다
land 땅	**bridge** 다리	**palace** 궁전	**capital** 수도	**address** 주소, 주소를 쓰디
structure 구조, 구조물	**resource** 자원	 **enter** 들어가다	**arrive** 도착하다	**free** 무료의, 자유로운
 **true** 사실인, 진짜의	**design** 디자인하다, 설계하다	**deliver** 배달하다	**policy** 정책, 방침	**limit** 제한하다, 제한, 한도

Day
11~15

맞힌 개수 : ___ / 40

❶ restaurant		㉑ 코미디, 희극	
❷ shop		㉒ 극장	
❸ after		㉓ 끔찍한, 형편없는	
❹ before		㉔ 특별한	
❺ cinema		㉕ 중앙, 가운데의	
❻ concert		㉖ 화면	
❼ sound		㉗ (극장 등의 좌석) 줄	
❽ depend		㉘ 앞쪽의, 앞면	
❾ sell		㉙ 거울	
❿ customer		㉚ 가격	
⓫ slide		㉛ 현금, 돈	
⓬ check		㉜ 상품	
⓭ live		㉝ 수도	
⓮ land		㉞ 주소, 주소를 쓰다	
⓯ bridge		㉟ 구조, 구조물	
⓰ palace		㊱ 자원	
⓱ design		㊲ 들어가다	
⓲ arrive		㊳ 배달하다	
⓳ free		㊴ 정책, 방침	
⓴ limit		㊵ 사실인, 진짜의	

Part 4

FINISH

START

Day 16 Human Diversity

Check Up Read and check the words you don't know.

1차 복습

- [ ] enter
- [ ] arrive
- [ ] free
- [ ] true
- [ ] design
- [ ] deliver
- [ ] policy
- [ ] limit

2차 복습

- [ ] sell
- [ ] customer
- [ ] slide
- [ ] goods

3차 복습

- [ ] explore
- [ ] alone
- [ ] countryside
- [ ] challenge

※ 망각 제로! 1일 전 3일 전 7일 전 학습한 단어를 복습해요.

Word Tip

enter 들어가다	arrive 도착하다	free 무료의, 자유로운	true 사실인, 진짜의
design 디자인하다, 설계하다	deliver 배달하다	policy 정책, 방침	limit 제한하다, 제한, 한도
sell 팔다	customer 손님, 고객	slide 미끄럼틀, 미끄러지다	goods 상품
explore 탐험하다	alone 혼자	countryside 시골 지역	challenge 도전, 도전하다

112

The movie was so exciting!

It's a movie where humans and apes
fight a war.

☐ 인종

그건 _____과 유인원이 전쟁을 벌이는 영화예요.

☐ 인간

Humans and apes evolved.

☐ 진화하다

인간과 유인원은 _____.

☐ 관련시키다

113

 Listen, say, and color.

 Write the **Basic Words** and **Jump Up Words**.

cousin 사촌	**My cousin is of a different race.** ⓝ 나의 사촌은 다른 인종이에요. _____ - - - - - - - - - - - - - - _____
human 인간, 인간의	**Humans are still looking for life on Mars.** ⓝ ⓐ 인간은 여전히 화성에서 생명체를 찾고 있어요. _____ - - - - - - - - - - - - - - _____
race 인종, 종족	**How many races are there in the world?** ⓝ 이 세상에는 얼마나 다양한 인종이 있나요? _____ - - - - - - - - - - - - - - _____ 

war
전쟁

The war separated many families. (n)

그 전쟁으로 많은 가족들이 헤어졌어요.

---

large
큰

He is a large man. (a)

그는 몸집이 큰 사람이에요.

---

identical
동일한, 똑같은

Her dress is almost identical to mine. (a)

그녀의 드레스는 내 것과 거의 똑같아요.

---

evolve
진화하다

Humans evolved over time. (v)

인간은 오랜 시간 동안 진화했어요.

---

relate
관련시키다,
관계시키다

Group work helps children relate to each other. (v)

그룹 활동은 아이들이 서로 관계를 형성하도록 도와줘요.

A Choose and write the words.

large	race	identical

1 인종, 종족

2 큰

3 동일한, 똑같은

B Choose and write the words.

cousin	human	evolve	relate

1 진화하다

2 사촌

3 관련시키다, 관계시키다

4 인간, 인간의

116

C Unscramble and complete the sentences.

1 그 전쟁으로 많은 가족들이 헤어졌어요.

w r a

The _____ separated many families.

2 그녀의 드레스는 내 것과 거의 똑같아요.

i d t c a l e n i

Her dress is almost _____ to mine.

3 나의 사촌은 다른 인종이에요.

i c u s o n

My _____ is of a different race.

D Choose and complete the sentences.

races   evolved   large

1 인간은 오랜 시간 동안 진화했어요.

Humans _____ over time.

2 이 세상에는 얼마나 다양한 인종이 있나요?

How many _____ are there in the world?

3 그는 몸집이 큰 사람이에요.

He is a _____ man.

Day 17 Grocery Shopping

Check Up Read and check the words you don't know.

1차 복습

- ☐ cousin
- ☐ race
- ☐ human
- ☐ war
- ☐ large
- ☐ evolve
- ☐ identical
- ☐ relate

2차 복습

- ☐ live
- ☐ land
- ☐ structure
- ☐ resource

3차 복습

- ☐ comedy
- ☐ theater
- ☐ after
- ☐ before

※ 망각 제로! 1일 전 3일 전 7일 전 학습한 단어를 복습해요.

Word Tip

cousin 사촌	race 인종, 종족	human 인간, 인간의	war 전쟁
large 큰	evolve 진화하다	identical 동일한, 똑같은	relate 관련시키다, 관계시키다
live 살다	land 땅	structure 구조, 구조물	resource 자원
comedy 코미디, 희극	theater 극장	after (시간상으로) 뒤에, 후에	before (시간상으로) 전에, 앞에

Dennis went grocery shopping.

데니스는 아빠와 식료품을 사러 갔어요.
Dennis went grocery shopping with his dad.

제가 카트 밀어 볼래요!
I want to push the cart!

그래.

데니스, 이거 무게 좀 달아 줄래?
Can you weigh this for me?

네~

scale

다 산 것 같군.
계산하러 가자.

으아!
줄이 엄청 길어요!

line

grocery list

4

Pop Quiz Choose and check the right words.

Dennis went grocery shopping with his dad.

데니스는 아빠와 _____ 쇼핑을 갔어요.

□ 식료품

□ 저울

Dennis wants to push the cart.

데니스는 _____ 를 밀고 싶어요.

□ 목록

□ 카트

 **Listen, say, and color.**

 Write the Basic Words and Jump Up Words.

cart 카트	**My dad is pushing a cart.** 우리 아빠가 카트를 밀고 있어요.

weigh 무게를 달다	**Let me weigh the bananas.** 바나나 무게를 달아볼게요.

push 밀다	**I pushed the door open.** 나는 그 문을 밀어서 열었어요.

near
가까운, 가까이

The market is near my house. (a) (adv)

그 시장은 우리 집에서 가까워요.

_____

_____

_____

line
줄, 선

This line is cash only.

이 줄은 현금만 받아요.

_____

_____

_____

scale
저울

The scale is used to weigh vegetables. (n)

저울은 채소의 무게를 재는 데 사용돼요.

_____

_____

_____

grocery
식료품

We went grocery shopping yesterday. (n)

우리는 어제 식료품 쇼핑을 했어요.

_____

_____

_____

list
목록, 리스트

Write a list of the food we need. (n)

우리에게 필요한 음식 목록을 작성하세요.

_____

_____

_____

A Find, circle, and write the words.

1

s c a l e i r t

저울

2

g r o c e r y b

식료품

3

v d n e a r z i

가까운, 가까이

4

u y l i n e x z

줄, 선

B Cross out, unscramble, and write the words.

1 카트

a h c r t

---

2 밀다

s p h e u

---

3 무게를 달다

e h i g t w

---

4 목록, 리스트

l m s t i

C Connect and fill in the blanks.

1

My dad is pushing a cart.

우리 아빠가 _____를 밀고 있어요.

2

Let me weigh the bananas.

바나나 _____ 볼게요.

3

Write a list of the food we need.

우리에게 필요한 음식 _____을 작성하세요.

D Rearrange and write the sentences.

1 이 줄은 현금만 받아요.

| line | only | cash | This | is | . |

_____

_____

_____

2 그 시장은 우리 집에서 가까워요.

| near | house | is | my | The market | . |

_____

_____

_____

Day 18 Water Parks

Check UP Read and check the words you don't know.

1차 복습

- ☐ cart
- ☐ weigh
- ☐ push
- ☐ near

- ☐ line
- ☐ scale
- ☐ grocery
- ☐ list

2차 복습

- ☐ enter
- ☐ arrive

- ☐ policy
- ☐ limit

3차 복습

- ☐ sound
- ☐ front

- ☐ middle
- ☐ screen

※망각 제로! 1일 전 3일 전 7일 전 학습한 단어를 복습해요.

Word Tip

cart 카트
line 줄, 선
enter 들어가다
sound 소리, 연주

weigh 무게를 달다
scale 저울
arrive 도착하다
front 앞쪽의, 앞면

push 밀다
grocery 식료품
policy 정책, 방침
middle 중앙, 가운데의

near 가까운, 가까이
list 목록, 리스트
limit 제한하다, 제한, 한도
screen 화면

124

We had fun at the water park.

Pop Quiz Choose and check the right words.

Dennis and his friends are at a huge water park.

데니스와 친구들이 _____ 물놀이장에 있어요.

☐ 깊은

☐ 거대한

The kids swimming pool is too shallow.

어린아이용 수영장은 너무 _____요.

☐ 어린

☐ 얕은

Listen, say, and color.

Write the Basic Words and Jump Up Words.

deep 깊은	**The swimming pool is deep.** _a 그 수영장은 깊어요. _____ - _____

chance 기회, 가능성	**This is our last chance to go on vacation this year.** _n 이번이 올해 휴가를 갈 수 있는 마지막 기회예요. _____ - _____

crowd 사람들, 군중	**A crowd soon gathered.** _n 사람들이 곧 몰려들었어요. _____ - _____ _____

away 떨어져	**The water park is a mile away.** *adv* 물놀이장은 1마일 떨어진 곳에 있어요.	
little 어린, 작은	**Little kids are not allowed in this pool.** *a* 어린아이들은 이 수영장에 들어갈 수 없어요.	
garage 주차장, 차고	**There is a large garage near the water park.** *n* 물놀이장 근처에 큰 주차장이 있어요.	
shallow 얕은	**The kids are playing in the shallow end.** *a* 그 아이들은 얕은 수심에서 놀고 있어요.	
huge 거대한	**The wave pool creates huge waves.** *a* 그 파도풀은 거대한 파도를 만들어요.	

A Choose and write the words.

deep   garage   chance

1

2

3

기회, 가능성   깊은   주차장, 차고

B Choose and write the words.

little   crowd   away   shallow

1 사람들, 군중

2 어린, 작은

3 얕은

4 떨어져

C Connect and fill in the blanks.

1

Little **kids** are not **allowed** in this pool.

_____ 아이들은 이 수영장에 들어갈 수 없어요.

2

The kids are playing in the **shallow** end.

그 아이들은 _____ 수심에서 놀고 있어요.

3

The wave pool creates huge **waves**.

그 파도풀은 _____ 파도를 만들어요.

D Rearrange and write the sentences.

1 사람들이 곧 몰려들었어요.

| gathered | soon | crowd | A | . |

_____

_____

_____

2 그 수영장은 깊어요.

| is | The | swimming | pool | deep | . |

_____

_____

_____

Day 19 Healthy Life

Check Up Read and check the words you don't know.

1차 복습

- [ ] deep
- [ ] chance
- [ ] crowd
- [ ] away

- [ ] little
- [ ] garage
- [ ] shallow
- [ ] huge

2차 복습

- [ ] cousin
- [ ] human

- [ ] evolve
- [ ] relate

3차 복습

- [ ] cash
- [ ] check

- [ ] mirror
- [ ] price

※ 망각 제로! 1일 전 3일 전 7일 전 학습한 단어를 복습해요.

 Word Tip

deep 깊은	chance 기회, 가능성	crowd 사람들, 군중	away 떨어져
little 어린, 작은	garage 주차장, 차고	shallow 얕은	huge 거대한
cousin 사촌	human 인간, 인간의	evolve 진화하다	relate 관련시키다, 관계시키다
cash 현금, 돈	check 확인하다	mirror 거울	price 가격

Dennis is into running these days.

Pop Quiz Choose and check the right words.

Dennis runs almost every day.

데니스는 _____ 매일 달려요.

☐ 거의

☐ 모든

Dennis's goal is to finish the marathon.

데니스의 _____는 마라톤 완주예요.

☐ 피부

☐ 목표

Catch Up

 **Listen & Say** Listen, say, and color.

Read & Write Write the **Basic Words** and **Jump Up Words**.

heart 심장	**Her heart is beating fast.** (n) 그녀의 심장이 빠르게 뛰고 있어요.

skin 피부	**My skin burns easily.** (n) 내 피부는 햇볕에 잘 타요.

almost 거의	**You are almost at the finish line.** (adv) 당신은 거의 결승점에 도달했어요. 

every
모든

I try to go running every morning. ^{det}

나는 매일 아침 뛰려고 노력해요.

---

goal
목표

I set goals for my health. ⁿ

나는 건강을 위해 목표를 세웠어요.

---

soak
담그다, 담기다

She soaked her feet in warm water. ^v

그녀는 따뜻한 물에 발을 담갔어요.

---

stomach
(신체) 배, 위

His stomach was full. ⁿ

그의 배는 가득 찼어요.

---

regular
규칙적인

Do you get regular exercise? ^a

당신은 규칙적인 운동을 하나요?

A Choose and write the words.

every	heart	soak

1

심장

2

모든

3

담그다, 담기다

B Choose and write the words.

skin	almost	stomach	regular

1 규칙적인

2 피부

3 거의

4 (신체) 배, 위

C Unscramble and complete the sentences.

1   나는 건강을 위해 목표를 세웠어요.   o g l a s

I set _____ for my health.

2   내 피부는 햇볕에 잘 타요.   s n i k

My _____ burns easily.

3   그녀의 심장이 빠르게 뛰고 있어요.   a h r e t

Her _____ is beating fast.

D Choose and complete the sentences.

regular   almost   soaked

1 당신은 거의 결승전에 도달했어요.

You are _____ at the finish line.

2 그녀는 따뜻한 물에 발을 담갔어요.

She _____ her feet in warm water.

3 당신은 규칙적인 운동을 하나요?

Do you get _____ exercise?

Day 20 Eating

Check Up Read and check the words you don't know.

1차 복습

- [ ] heart
- [ ] skin
- [ ] almost
- [ ] every
- [ ] goal
- [ ] soak
- [ ] stomach
- [ ] regular

2차 복습

- [ ] cart
- [ ] weigh
- [ ] grocery
- [ ] list

3차 복습

- [ ] bridge
- [ ] palace
- [ ] capital
- [ ] address

※ **망각 제로!** 1일 전 3일 전 7일 전 학습한 단어를 복습해요.

Word Tip

heart 심장	skin 피부	almost 거의	every 모든
goal 목표	soak 담그다, 담기다	stomach (신체) 배, 위	regular 규칙적인
cart 카트	weigh 무게를 달다	grocery 식료품	list 목록, 리스트
bridge 다리	palace 궁전	capital 수도	address 주소, 주소를 쓰다

Rod doesn't like beans.

Pop Quiz Choose and check the right words.

It's Rod's suppertime.

로드네 _____ 시간이에요.

Beans are rich in fiber.

_____은 섬유질이 풍부해요.

☐ 섬유질

☐ 저녁 (식사)

☐ 콩

☐ 원천

Catch Up

supper
저녁 (식사)

She made a big supper for her family.

그녀는 가족을 위해 풍성한 저녁 식사를 준비했어요.

bean
콩

He loves all kinds of beans.

그는 모든 종류의 콩을 좋아해요.

plan
계획, 계획하다

My plan is to cook steak tonight.

내 계획은 오늘 밤에 스테이크를 요리하는 거예요.

hope
희망하다, 희망

I hope to take her out for dinner. (v n)

나는 그녀와 저녁 식사하러 가길 바라요.

_____

_____

_____

soft
부드러운

He can eat only soft food. (a)

그는 부드러운 음식만 먹을 수 있어요.

_____

_____

_____

fiber
섬유, 섬유질

Fruit peels contain dietary fiber. (n)

과일 껍질은 식이 섬유를 함유하고 있어요.

_____

_____

_____

source
원천, 근원

Milk is a good source of protein. (n)

우유는 단백질의 훌륭한 공급원이에요.

_____

_____

_____

refuse
거부하다,
거절하다

He refuses to waste food. (v)

그는 음식 낭비하는 것을 거부해요.

_____

_____

_____

A Find, circle, and write the words.

1 m s u p p e r l

저녁 (식사)

2 q e s o u r c e p

원천, 근원

3 a q r e f u s e

거부하다,
거절하다

4 v p l a n c y t

계획,
계획하다

B Cross out, unscramble, and write the words.

1 콩   p e a n b

2 섬유, 섬유질   g b r i f e

3 부드러운   f s o w t

4 희망하다, 희망   e o z h p

C Connect and fill in the blanks.

1

He loves all kinds of beans.

그는 모든 종류의 _____을 좋아해요.

2

He can eat only soft food.

그는 _____ 음식만 먹을 수 있어요.

3

My plan is to cook steak tonight.

내 _____은 오늘 밤에 스테이크를 요리하는 거예요.

D Rearrange and write the sentences.

1 그는 음식 낭비하는 것을 거부해요.

| He | food | to | refuses | waste | . |

_____

- -

_____

2 과일 껍질은 식이 섬유를 함유하고 있어요.

| contain | fiber | Fruit peels | dietary | . |

_____

- -

_____

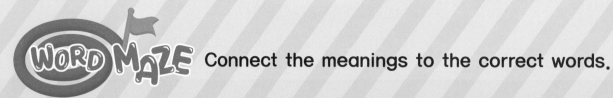

WORD MAZE

Connect the meanings to the correct words.

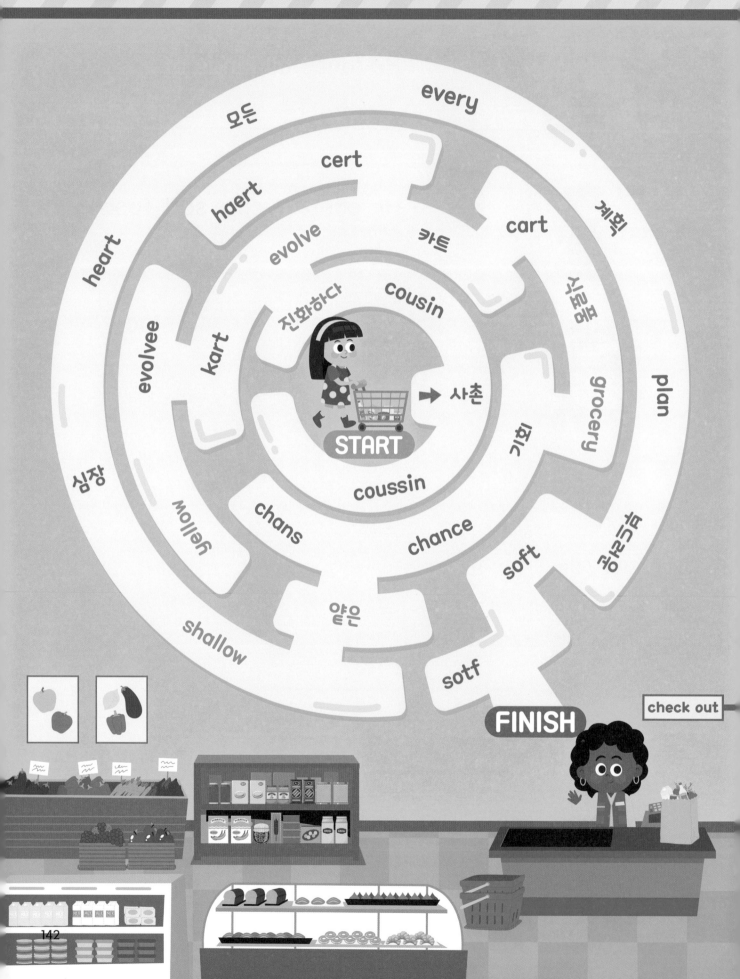

every
모든
cert
haert
cart
heart
evolve
계획
카트
cousin
식료품
진화하다
grocery
evolvee
kart
plan
START → 사촌
심장
coussin
계획
yellow
chans
chance
soft
할인판매
얕은
shallow
sotf

FINISH

check out

cousin 사촌	**human** 인간, 인간의	**race** 인종, 종족	**war** 전쟁	**large** 큰
identical 동일한, 똑같은	**evolve** 진화하다	**relate** 관련시키다, 관계시키다	**cart** 카트	**weigh** 무게를 달다
push 밀다	**near** 가까운, 가까이	**line** 줄, 선	**scale** 저울	**grocery** 식료품
list 목록, 리스트	**deep** 깊은	**chance** 기회, 가능성	**crowd** 사람들, 군중	**away** 떨어져
little 어린, 작은	**garage** 주차장, 차고	**shallow** 얕은	**huge** 거대한	**heart** 심장
skin 피부	**almost** 거의	**every** 모든	**goal** 목표	**soak** 담그다, 담기다
stomach (신체) 배, 위	**regular** 규칙적인	**supper** 저녁 (식사)	**bean** 콩	**plan** 계획, 계획하다
hope 희망하다, 희망	**soft** 부드러운	**fiber** 섬유, 섬유질	**source** 원천, 근원	**refuse** 거부하다, 거절하다

Day 16~20

맞힌 개수 : ☐ / 40

❶ cousin		㉑ 큰	
❷ human		㉒ 인종, 종족	
❸ identical		㉓ 진화하다	
❹ relate		㉔ 전쟁	
❺ cart		㉕ 줄, 선	
❻ weigh		㉖ 저울	
❼ push		㉗ 식료품	
❽ near		㉘ 목록, 리스트	
❾ deep		㉙ 어린, 작은	
❿ chance		㉚ 주차장, 차고	
⓫ crowd		㉛ 얕은	
⓬ away		㉜ 거대한	
⓭ heart		㉝ 목표	
⓮ soak		㉞ 피부	
⓯ almost		㉟ (신체) 배, 위	
⓰ every		㊱ 규칙적인	
⓱ supper		㊲ 부드러운	
⓲ refuse		㊳ 섬유, 섬유질	
⓳ plan		㊴ 원천, 근원	
⓴ hope		㊵ 콩	

Part 5

FINISH

START

Day 21 Travel

1차 복습

- ☐ supper
- ☐ bean
- ☐ plan
- ☐ hope
- ☐ soft
- ☐ fiber
- ☐ source
- ☐ refuse

2차 복습

- ☐ deep
- ☐ chance
- ☐ shallow
- ☐ huge

3차 복습

- ☐ free
- ☐ true
- ☐ design
- ☐ deliver

※ 망각 제로! 1일 전 3일 전 7일 전 학습한 단어를 복습해요.

Word Tip

supper 저녁 (식사)	**bean** 콩	**plan** 계획, 계획하다	**hope** 희망하다, 희망
soft 부드러운	**fiber** 섬유, 섬유질	**source** 원천, 근원	**refuse** 거부하다, 거절하다
deep 깊은	**chance** 기회, 가능성	**shallow** 얕은	**huge** 거대한
free 무료의, 자유로운	**true** 사실인, 진짜의	**design** 디자인하다, 설계하다	**deliver** 배달하다

146

Which seat do you prefer on the plane?

POP Quiz Choose and check the right words.

Kiara's dad booked their flights yesterday.
키아라의 아빠가 어제 _____을 예약했어요.

- [ ] 출구
- [ ] 항공편

Sally prefers aisle seats.
샐리는 통로 _____을 선호해요.

- [ ] 좌석
- [ ] 엔진

Read & Write Write the **Basic Words** and **Jump Up Words**.

board 탑승하다	**Let's board our flight.** v 비행기를 타러 가자. _____ - _____

captain 선장, 기장	**The captain took the wheel of the ship.** n 선장이 배의 키를 잡았어요. _____ - _____

engine 엔진	**We need to look at the engine.** n 우리는 엔진을 살펴봐야 해요. _____ - _____

exit
출구

Where is the exit?

출구가 어디예요?

---

speed
속도

The car was gathering speed.

그 차는 속도를 올리기 시작했어요.

---

flight
항공편, 비행

I will book a flight on the Internet.

나는 인터넷으로 항공편을 예약할 거예요.

---

seat
좌석

Please return to your seat.

자리로 돌아가 주세요.

---

sign
표지판, 표시

The sign says 'Do Not Enter.'

'들어가지 마시오.'라고 표지판에 쓰여 있어요.

A Choose and write the words.

exit	seat	flight

1

_____

좌석

2

_____

출구

3

_____

항공편, 비행

B Choose and write the words.

speed	sign	engine	board

1 탑승하다

_____ _____

2 표지판, 표시

_____ _____

3 엔진

_____ _____

4 속도

_____ _____

C Connect and fill in the blanks.

1.
We need to look at the engine.

우리는 ＿＿＿＿＿＿＿을 살펴봐야 해요.

2.
The car was gathering speed.

그 차는 ＿＿＿＿＿＿＿를 올리기 시작했어요.

3.
The sign **says 'Do Not Enter.'**

'들어가지 마시오.'라고 ＿＿＿＿＿＿＿에 쓰여 있어요.

D Rearrange and write the sentences.

1. 출구가 어디예요?

| Where | exit | the | is | ? |

2. 비행기를 타러 가자.

| flight | our | board | Let's | . |

Check UP   Read and check the words you don't know.

1차 복습

- [ ] board
- [ ] captain
- [ ] engine
- [ ] exit

- [ ] speed
- [ ] flight
- [ ] seat
- [ ] sign

2차 복습

- [ ] heart
- [ ] skin

- [ ] stomach
- [ ] regular

3차 복습

- [ ] race
- [ ] war

- [ ] large
- [ ] identical

※ 망각 제로! 1일 전 3일 전 7일 전 학습한 단어를 복습해요.

Word Tip

board 탑승하다	**captain** 선장, 기장	**engine** 엔진	**exit** 출구
speed 속도	**flight** 항공편, 비행	**seat** 좌석	**sign** 표지판, 표시
heart 심장	**skin** 피부	**stomach** (신체) 배, 위	**regular** 규칙적인
race 인종, 종족	**war** 전쟁	**large** 큰	**identical** 동일한, 똑같은

Have you ever donated blood?

Pop Quiz Choose and check the right words.

Rod donated blood two weeks ago.

로드는 2주 _____ 헌혈을 했어요.

☐ 전에

☐ 일주일

Rod got lots of rest after donating blood.

로드는 헌혈 후에 충분한 _____을 취했어요.

☐ 혜택

☐ 휴식

blood
피, 혈액

He donated blood last week.

그는 지난주에 헌혈했어요

---

week
일주일, 주

She volunteers at the library every week.

그녀는 매주 도서관에서 봉사 활동을 해요.

---

type
종류, 유형

What is your blood type?

당신의 혈액형은 무엇이에요?

collect
모으다

They collect clothes for the poor. *(v)*

그들은 가난한 사람들을 위해 옷을 모아요.

---

ago
(지금으로부터)
전에

I helped take care of animals two years ago. *(adv)*

나는 2년 전에 동물들을 돌보는 것을 도왔어요.

---

donate
기부하다,
기증하다

I often donate money to charity. *(v)*

나는 종종 자선 단체에 돈을 기부해요.

---

rest
휴식, 쉬다

You should take a rest. *(n)(v)*

당신은 휴식을 취해야 해요.

---

benefit
혜택, 이점

There are many benefits to volunteer work. *(n)*

봉사 활동에는 많은 이점이 있어요

A Choose and write the words.

rest	benefit	blood

1

혜택, 이점

2

휴식, 쉬다

3

피, 혈액

B Choose and write the words.

type	week	collect	donate

1 일주일, 주

2 모으다

3 종류, 유형

4 기부하다, 기증하다

C Unscramble and complete the sentences.

1 당신은 휴식을 취해야 해요.

r t s e

You should take a _____ .

2 당신의 혈액형은 무엇이에요?

p t e y

What is your blood _____ ?

3 그녀는 매주 도서관에서 봉사 활동을 해요.

k w e e

She volunteers at the library every

_____ .

D Choose and complete the sentences.

collect   ago   benefits

1 나는 2년 전에 동물들을 돌보는 것을 도왔어요.

I helped take care of animals two years _____ .

2 그들은 가난한 사람들을 위해 옷을 모아요.

They _____ clothes for the poor.

3 봉사 활동에는 많은 이점이 있어요.

There are many _____ to volunteer work.

Day 23 Sports

Check Up Read and check the words you don't know.

1차 복습

- [ ] blood
- [ ] week
- [ ] type
- [ ] collect
- [ ] ago
- [ ] donate
- [ ] rest
- [ ] benefit

2차 복습

- [ ] supper
- [ ] bean
- [ ] source
- [ ] refuse

3차 복습

- [ ] push
- [ ] near
- [ ] line
- [ ] scale

※ 망각 제로! 1일 전 3일 전 7일 전 학습한 단어를 복습해요.

 **Word Tip**

blood 피, 혈액	week 일주일, 주	type 종류, 유형	collect 모으다
ago (지금으로부터) 전에	donate 기부하다, 기증하다	rest 휴식, 쉬다	benefit 혜택, 이점
supper 저녁 (식사)	bean 콩	source 원천, 근원	refuse 거부하다, 거절하다
push 밀다	near 가까운, 가까이	line 중앙, 가운데의	scale 저울

Indoor rock climbing is fun!

Pop Quiz Choose and check the right words.

The indoor rock climbing wall is high.

실내 암벽은 _____요.

☐ 높은

☐ 멀리

Dennis has already climbed that far.

데니스는 벌써 저 멀리 _____.

☐ 가능한

☐ 오르다

 Write the **Basic Words** and **Jump Up Words**.

climb 오르다	**She likes to climb mountains.** 그녀는 산에 올라가는 것을 좋아해요. _____

v

mind 마음	**Yoga relaxes the mind.** 요가는 마음을 편안하게 해 줘요. _____

n

high 높은, 높이가 ~인	**How high is Mount Everest?** 에베레스트산은 높이가 얼마인가요? _____

a

possible
가능한

It is possible for us to win. [a]

우리가 이기는 것은 가능해요.

---

far
멀리

Throw this ball as far as you can. [adv]

이 공을 멀리 던질 수 있는 데까지 던져 봐요.

---

rope
밧줄

Hold on tight to the rope. [n]

밧줄을 꽉 잡으세요.

---

dynamic
역동적인

This sport is so dynamic. [a]

이 스포츠는 매우 역동적이에요.

---

muscle
근육

Daily exercise keeps your muscles strong. [n]

매일 하는 운동은 근육을 강하게 유지해 줘요.

A Choose and write the words.

possible	mind	muscle

1

_____
_____
_____

마음

2

_____
_____
_____

근육

3

_____
_____
_____

가능한

B Choose and write the words.

climb	high	rope	far

1 밧줄

_____
_____
_____

2 오르다

_____
_____
_____

3 높이, 높이가 ~인

_____
_____
_____

4 멀리

_____
_____
_____

C Connect and fill in the blanks.

1

How high is Mount Everest?

에베레스트산은 _____가 얼마인가요?

2

This sport is so dynamic.

이 스포츠는 매우 _____이에요.

3

Hold on tight to the rope.

_____을 꽉 잡으세요.

D Rearrange and write the sentences.

1 요가는 마음을 편안하게 해 줘요.

| the | Yoga | relaxes | mind | . |

_____

2 그녀는 산에 올라가는 것을 좋아해요.

| She | climb | to | mountains | likes | . |

_____

Day 24 Animals

Check Up Read and check the words you don't know.

1차 복습

☐ climb   ☐ far

☐ mind   ☐ rope

☐ high   ☐ dynamic

☐ possible   ☐ muscle

2차 복습

☐ board   ☐ seat

☐ captain   ☐ sign

3차 복습

☐ crowd   ☐ little

☐ away   ☐ garage

※ 망각 제로! 1일 전 3일 전 7일 전 학습한 단어를 복습해요.

Word Tip

climb 오르다	mind 마음	high 높은, 높이가 ~인	possible 가능한
far 멀리	rope 밧줄	dynamic 역동적인	muscle 근육
board 탑승하다	captain 선장, 기장	seat 좌석	sign 표지판, 표시
crowd 사람들, 군중	away 떨어져	little 어린, 작은	garage 주차장, 차고

Cats have rough tongues.

Pop Quiz Choose and check the right words.

Luna's tongue is rough!

루나의 _____는 거칠어요.

- [ ] 혀
- [ ] 꼬리

Cats' tongues are covered with tiny spines.

고양이의 혀는 _____ 가시들로 덮여 있어요.

- [ ] 아주 작은
- [ ] 거친

Catch Up

Listen, say, and color.

Write the **Basic Words** and **Jump Up Words**.

tail 꼬리	**A dog is wagging its tail.** 개가 꼬리를 흔들고 있어요.

bone 뼈	**The deer has broken a bone in its leg.** 그 사슴은 다리뼈가 부러졌어요.

dolphin 돌고래	**The dolphin is an intelligent animal.** 돌고래는 영리한 동물이에요.

fox
여우

There is a fox in the forest. (n)

숲에 여우가 있어요.

copy
따라 하다,
복사하다

The puppies copy everything their mom does. (v)

그 강아지들은 엄마가 하는 모든 것을 따라 해요.

rough
거친

It has a hard and rough skin. (a)

그 피부는 딱딱하고 거칠어요.

tongue
혀

The giraffe has a long tongue. (n)

그 기린은 긴 혀를 가지고 있어요.

tiny
아주 작은

The kitten's feet are so tiny. (a)

새끼 고양이의 발은 아주 작아요.

A Choose and write the words.

dolphin	fox	bone

1

여우

2

뼈

3

돌고래

B Choose and write the words.

tail	rough	copy	tongue

1 꼬리

2 혀

3 거친

4 따라 하다, 복사하다

C Unscramble and complete the sentences.

1
숲에 여우가 있어요.

o x f

There is a _____ in the forest.

2
개가 꼬리를 흔들고 있어요.

l t a i

A dog is wagging its _____.

3
그 피부는 딱딱하고 거칠어요.

o g r h u

It has a hard and _____ skin.

D Choose and complete the sentences.

bone   tiny   dolphin

1 그 사슴은 다리뼈가 부러졌어요.

The deer has broken a _____ in its leg.

2 돌고래는 영리한 동물이에요.

The _____ is an intelligent animal.

3 새끼 고양이의 발은 아주 작아요.

The kitten's feet are so _____.

Day 25 Daily Life & Healthy Habits

Check Up Read and check the words you don't know.

- ☐ tail
- ☐ bone
- ☐ dolphin
- ☐ fox
- ☐ copy
- ☐ rough
- ☐ tongue
- ☐ tiny

- ☐ blood
- ☐ week
- ☐ rest
- ☐ benefit

- ☐ almost
- ☐ every
- ☐ goal
- ☐ soak

※ 망각 제로! 1일 전 3일 전 7일 전 학습한 단어를 복습해요.

Word Tip

tail 꼬리	bone 뼈	dolphin 돌고래	fox 여우
copy 따라 하다, 복사하다	rough 거친	tongue 혀	tiny 아주 작은
blood 피, 혈액	week 일주일, 주	rest 휴식, 쉬다	benefit 혜택, 이점
almost 거의	every 모든	goal 목표	soak 담그다, 담기다

Sally wants to sleep well.

Pop Quiz Choose and check the right words.

It's better that the mattress is not too hard.

매트리스는 너무 _____ 않은 것이 좋아요.

☐ 단단한

☐ 밝은

Take a deep breath and relax.

심호흡을 해서 _____.

☐ 긴장을 풀다

☐ 향상시키다

 **Listen, say, and color.**

 Write the Basic Words and Jump Up Words.

---

hard
단단한, 딱딱한

A hard mattress is better for you. ⓐ

당신에게는 단단한 매트리스가 더 좋아요.

_____

_____

---

bright
밝은

It's too bright to sleep. ⓐ

잠을 자기에 너무 밝아요.

_____

_____

---

curtain
커튼

Close the curtains before you sleep. ⓝ

자기 전에 커튼을 닫아요.

_____

_____

---

habit
습관

Exercising daily is a good habit. n

매일 운동하는 것은 좋은 습관이에요.

cool
시원한, 서늘한

The fan keeps my room cool. a

선풍기는 내 방을 시원하게 해 줘요.

relax
긴장을 풀다,
느긋이 쉬다

Sit back and relax. v

등을 기대고 긴장을 풀어요.

breathe
숨을 쉬다

Lie flat and breathe deeply. v

반듯이 누워서 깊게 숨을 쉬세요

improve
향상시키다,
개선하다

I need to improve my muscular strength. v

나는 근력을 향상시켜야 해요.

A Choose and write the words.

relax	breathe	cool

1

숨을 쉬다

2

시원한, 서늘한

3

긴장을 풀다, 느긋이 쉬다

B Choose and write the words.

hard	curtain	improve	habit

1 향상시키다, 개선하다

2 단단한, 딱딱한

3 습관

4 커튼

C Connect and fill in the blanks.

① Close the **curtains** before you sleep.

자기 전에 ＿＿＿＿＿＿＿을 닫아요.

② A **hard** mattress is better for you.

당신에게는 ＿＿＿＿＿＿＿ 매트리스가 더 좋아요.

③ Exercising daily is a good habit.

매일 운동하는 것은 좋은 ＿＿＿＿＿＿＿ 이에요.

D Rearrange and write the sentences.

① 등을 기대고 긴장을 풀어요.

| Sit | and | relax | back | . |

_____
_____
_____

② 잠을 자기에 너무 밝아요.

| to | too | sleep | It's | bright | . |

_____
_____
_____

WORD PUZZLE Complete the word puzzle.

ACROSS

① A _____ mattress is better for you.

③ You should take a _____.

⑥ She likes to _____ mountains.

⑧ I helped take care of animals two years _____.

⑨ There is a _____ in the forest.

DOWN

② Hold on tight to the _____.

④ Please return to your _____.

⑤ The _____ says 'Do Not Enter.'

⑥ The fan keeps my room _____.

⑦ The deer has broken a _____ in its leg.

board	captain	engine	exit	speed
탑승하다	선장, 기장	엔진	출구	속도

flight	seat	sign	blood	week
항공편, 비행	좌석	표지판, 표시	피, 혈액	일주일, 주

type	collect	ago	donate	rest
종류, 유형	모으다	(지금으로부터) 전에	기부하다, 기증하다	휴식, 쉬다

benefit	climb	mind	high	possible
혜택, 이점	오르다	마음	높은, 높이가 ~인	가능한

far	rope	dynamic	muscle	tail
멀리	밧줄	역동적인	근육	꼬리

bone	dolphin	fox	copy	rough
뼈	돌고래	여우	따라 하다, 복사하다	거친

tongue	tiny	hard	bright	curtain
혀	아주 작은	단단한, 딱딱한	밝은	커튼

habit	cool	relax	breathe	improve
습관	시원한, 서늘한	긴장을 풀다, 느긋이 쉬다	숨을 쉬다	향상시키다, 개선하다

Day
21~25

① board		㉑ 속도	
② captain		㉒ 항공편, 비행	
③ engine		㉓ 좌석	
④ exit		㉔ 표지판, 표시	
⑤ ago		㉕ 피, 혈액	
⑥ donate		㉖ 일주일, 주	
⑦ type		㉗ 휴식, 쉬다	
⑧ collect		㉘ 혜택, 이점	
⑨ climb		㉙ 멀리	
⑩ mind		㉚ 밧줄	
⑪ high		㉛ 역동적인	
⑫ possible		㉜ 근육	
⑬ tail		㉝ 돌고래	
⑭ bone		㉞ 거친	
⑮ copy		㉟ 혀	
⑯ fox		㊱ 아주 작은	
⑰ hard		㊲ 시원한, 서늘한	
⑱ relax		㊳ 밝은	
⑲ curtain		㊴ 숨을 쉬다	
⑳ habit		㊵ 향상시키다, 개선하다	

Answer Key

Level 3.1

Day 01

P11

POP Quiz ☑ 결혼식 ☐ 친척 ☑ 가까운 ☐ 정중한

P14~15

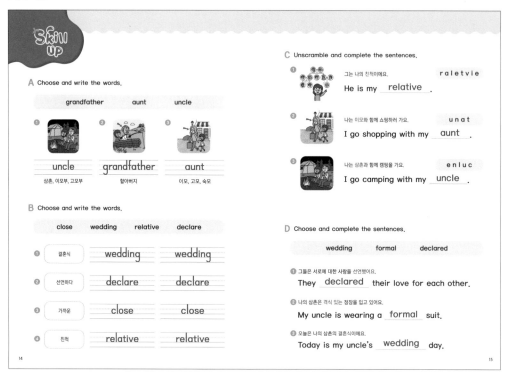

Skill UP

A Choose and write the words.

| grandfather | aunt | uncle |

① uncle
삼촌, 이모부, 고모부

② grandfather
할아버지

③ aunt
이모, 고모, 숙모

B Choose and write the words.

| close | wedding | relative | declare |

① 결혼식 — wedding — wedding
② 선언하다 — declare — declare
③ 가까운 — close — close
④ 친척 — relative — relative

C Unscramble and complete the sentences.

① 그는 나의 친척이에요.   raletvie
He is my relative .

② 나는 이모와 함께 쇼핑하러 가요.   unat
I go shopping with my aunt .

③ 나는 삼촌과 함께 캠핑을 가요.   enluc
I go camping with my uncle .

D Choose and complete the sentences.

| wedding | formal | declared |

① 그들은 서로에 대한 사랑을 선언했어요.
They declared their love for each other.

② 나의 삼촌은 격식 있는 정장을 입고 있어요.
My uncle is wearing a formal suit.

③ 오늘은 나의 삼촌의 결혼식이에요.
Today is my uncle's wedding day.

14   15

Day 02

P17

POP Quiz ☑ 반려동물 ☐ 그릇 ☐ 유지하다 ☑ 먹이를 주다

P20~21

Skill UP

A Find, circle, and write the words.

① 쥐 — a d m o u s e j h — mouse
② 강아지 — q p u p p y i u — puppy
③ 유지하다, 가지고 있다 — k e e p u i e t — keep
④ 그릇 — v e c t b o w l — bowl

B Cross out, unscramble, and write the words.

① 책임감 있는 — biresolpnsex — responsible
② 물다 — xeibt — bite
③ 먹이를 주다 — fxede — feed
④ 반려동물 — mtep — pet

C Connect and fill in the blanks.

① I feed my dog every morning.
나는 매일 아침 내 개에게 먹이를 줘요 .

② My puppy likes to bite.
나의 강아지는 무는 걸 좋아해요.

③ She is a responsible pet owner.
그녀는 책임감 있는 반려동물 주인이에요.

D Rearrange and write the sentences.

① 당신은 개 밥그릇을 깨끗하게 유지해야 해요.

| clean | should | the dog | You | keep | bowl | . |

You should keep the dog bowl clean.

② 그것은 반려용 쥐예요.

| It | a | pet | is | mouse | . |

It is a pet mouse.

20   21

Day 03

P23

 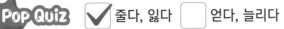 ✔ 줄다, 잃다 ☐ 얻다, 늘리다 ☐ 날씬한 ✔ 충분한

P26~27

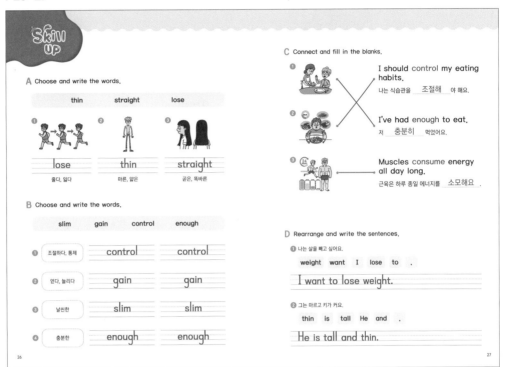

Skill UP

A Choose and write the words.

| thin | straight | lose |

❶ lose
줄다, 잃다

❷ thin
마른, 얇은

❸ straight
곧은, 똑바른

B Choose and write the words.

| slim | gain | control | enough |

❶ 조절하다, 통제 control control

❷ 얻다, 늘리다 gain gain

❸ 날씬한 slim slim

❹ 충분한 enough enough

C Connect and fill in the blanks.

❶ I should control my eating habits.
나는 식습관을 __조절해__ 야 해요.

❷ I've had enough to eat.
저 __충분히__ 먹었어요.

❸ Muscles consume energy all day long.
근육은 하루 종일 에너지를 __소모해요__ .

D Rearrange and write the sentences.

❶ 나는 살을 빼고 싶어요.

| weight | want | I | lose | to | . |

__I want to lose weight.__

❷ 그는 마르고 키가 커요.

| thin | is | tall | He | and | . |

__He is tall and thin.__

26   27

Day 04

P29

  ☐ 사냥하다 ✔ 살아남다 ☐ 동굴 ✔ 숲

P32~33

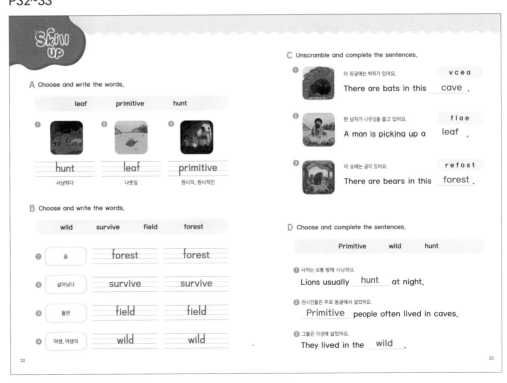

Skill UP

A Choose and write the words.

| leaf | primitive | hunt |

❶ hunt
사냥하다

❷ leaf
나뭇잎

❸ primitive
원시의, 원시적인

B Choose and write the words.

| wild | survive | field | forest |

❶ 숲 forest forest

❷ 살아남다 survive survive

❸ 들판 field field

❹ 야생, 야생의 wild wild

C Unscramble and complete the sentences.

❶ 이 동굴에는 박쥐가 있어요.   v c e a
There are bats in this cave .

❷ 한 남자가 나뭇잎을 줍고 있어요.   f l a e
A man is picking up a leaf .

❸ 이 숲에는 곰이 있어요.   r e f o s t
There are bears in this forest .

D Choose and complete the sentences.

| Primitive | wild | hunt |

❶ 사자는 보통 밤에 사냥해요.
Lions usually hunt at night.

❷ 원시인들은 주로 동굴에서 살았어요.
 Primitive people often lived in caves.

❸ 그들은 야생에 살았어요.
They lived in the wild .

32   33

Day 05

P35

 POP Quiz [ ] 단서 [✓] 쌍둥이 [✓] 같은 [ ] 다른

P38~39

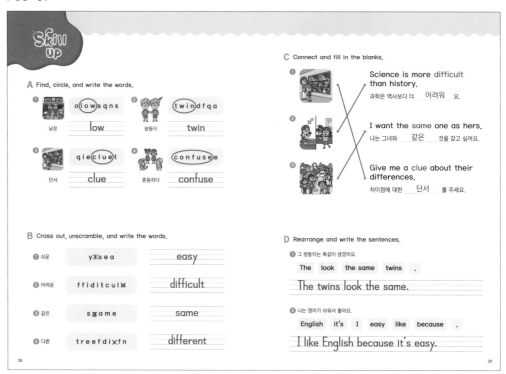

Skill Up

A Find, circle, and write the words.

① o l o w s q n s — 낮은 — low
② t w i n d f q a — 쌍둥이 — twin
③ q i e c l u e t — 단서 — clue
④ c o n f u s e e — 혼동하다 — confuse

B Cross out, unscramble, and write the words.

① 쉬운 — y x s e a — easy
② 어려운 — f f i d i t c u l x — difficult
③ 같은 — s x a m e — same
④ 다른 — t r e e f d i x f n — different

C Connect and fill in the blanks.

① Science is more difficult than history.
과학은 역사보다 더 <u>어려워</u> 요.

② I want the same one as hers.
나는 그녀와 <u>같은</u> 것을 갖고 싶어요.

③ Give me a clue about their differences.
차이점에 대한 <u>단서</u> 를 주세요.

D Rearrange and write the sentences.

① 그 쌍둥이는 똑같이 생겼어요.
The / look / the same / twins / .
The twins look the same.

② 나는 영어가 쉬워서 좋아요.
English / it's / I / easy / like / because / .
I like English because it's easy.

38   39

Day 01~05

P40   P42

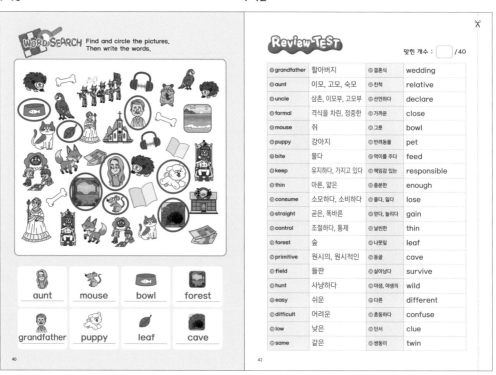

WORD SEARCH Find and circle the pictures. Then write the words.

aunt   mouse   bowl   forest

grandfather   puppy   leaf   cave

40

Review Test   맞힌 개수 : [   ] / 40

① grandfather	할아버지	㉑ 결혼식	wedding
② aunt	이모, 고모, 숙모	㉒ 친척	relative
③ uncle	삼촌, 이모부, 고모부	㉓ 선언하다	declare
④ formal	격식을 차린, 정중한	㉔ 가까운	close
⑤ mouse	쥐	㉕ 그릇	bowl
⑥ puppy	강아지	㉖ 반려동물	pet
⑦ bite	물다	㉗ 먹이를 주다	feed
⑧ keep	유지하다, 가지고 있다	㉘ 책임감 있는	responsible
⑨ thin	마른, 얇은	㉙ 충분한	enough
⑩ consume	소모하다, 소비하다	㉚ 줄다, 잃다	lose
⑪ straight	곧은, 똑바른	㉛ 얻다, 늘리다	gain
⑫ control	조절하다, 통제	㉜ 날씬한	thin
⑬ forest	숲	㉝ 나뭇잎	leaf
⑭ primitive	원시의, 원시적인	㉞ 동굴	cave
⑮ field	들판	㉟ 살아남다	survive
⑯ hunt	사냥하다	㊱ 야생, 야생의	wild
⑰ easy	쉬운	㊲ 다른	different
⑱ difficult	어려운	㊳ 혼동하다	confuse
⑲ low	낮은	㊴ 단서	clue
⑳ same	같은	㊵ 쌍둥이	twin

42

Day 06

P45

 ✓지구 ☐우주 ✓표면 ☐행성

P48~49

Skill Up

A Choose and write the words.

around	ground	ocean

① ocean
바다, 대양

② around
~ 주위에, 주변에

③ ground
땅

B Choose and write the words.

space	dot	surface	planet

① 표면 | surface | surface
② 점 | dot | dot
③ 행성 | planet | planet
④ 우주 | space | space

C Connect and fill in the blanks.

① The astrorant is exploring space.
우주 비행사는 __우주__ 를 탐험하고 있어요.

② My house looks like a dot on the map.
내 집은 지도에서 __점__ 처럼 보여요.

③ Water covers most of Earth's surface.
물은 지구 __표면__ 대부분을 덮고 있어요.

D Rearrange and write the sentences.

① 우리는 지구를 구해야 해요.
save   We   Earth   should   .
We should save Earth.

② 땅은 축축하고, 진흙투성이였어요.
was   and   wet   muddy   The   ground   .
The ground was wet and muddy.

48

49

Day 07

P51

 ☐퍼즐 ✓취미 ✓두뇌, 뇌 ☐주문

P54~55

Skill Up

A Choose and write the words.

side	brain	memory

① brain
두뇌, 뇌

② side
(좌우 절반 중 한) 쪽

③ memory
기억(력)

B Choose and write the words.

puzzle	order	relieve	hobby

① 퍼즐, 수수께끼 | puzzle | puzzle
② 취미 | hobby | hobby
③ 주문하다, 주문 | order | order
④ 없애 주다, 완화하다 | relieve | relieve

C Unscramble and complete the sentences.

① 그는 퍼즐을 맞추었어요.   pzluez
He put the __puzzle__ together.

② 입장권은 매표소에서 구할 수 있어요.   laavilabe
Tickets are __available__ from the box office.

③ 온라인으로 입장권을 주문하셨나요?   errod
Did you __order__ your tickets online?

D Choose and complete the sentences.

Memory	relieve	hobbies

① 기억력은 그 게임의 핵심이에요.
__Memory__ is the key point of the game.

② 내 취미 중의 하나는 사진 찍기예요.
One of my __hobbies__ is taking pictures.

③ 그건 스트레스 없애는 데 아주 좋은 방법이에요.
It's a very good way to __relieve__ stress.

54

55

Day 08

P57

POP QUIZ ☐ 교회 ☑ 묻다 ☐ 무덤 ☑ 믿다

P60~61

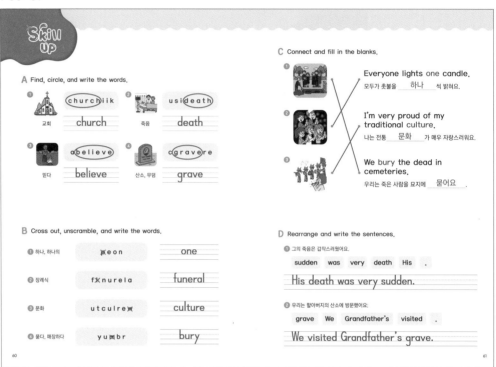

Skill UP

A Find, circle, and write the words.

1. (churchiik) → church (교회)
2. usideath → death (죽음)
3. abelieve → believe (믿다)
4. cgravere → grave (산소, 무덤)

B Cross out, unscramble, and write the words.

1. 하나, 하나의 — xeon — one
2. 장례식 — fxnurela — funeral
3. 문화 — utculrex — culture
4. 묻다, 매장하다 — yumbr — bury

C Connect and fill in the blanks.

1. Everyone lights one candle.
   모두가 촛불을 __하나__ 씩 밝혀요.
2. I'm very proud of my traditional culture.
   나는 전통 __문화__ 가 매우 자랑스러워요.
3. We bury the dead in cemeteries.
   우리는 죽은 사람을 묘지에 __묻어요__ .

D Rearrange and write the sentences.

1. 그의 죽음은 갑작스러웠어요.
   sudden was very death His .
   __His death was very sudden.__
2. 우리는 할아버지의 산소에 방문했어요.
   grave We Grandfather's visited .
   __We visited Grandfather's grave.__

60

61

Day 09

P63

POP QUIZ ☐ 점수 ☑ 시험 ☑ 몹시 싫어하다 ☐ (시험에) 떨어지다

P66~67

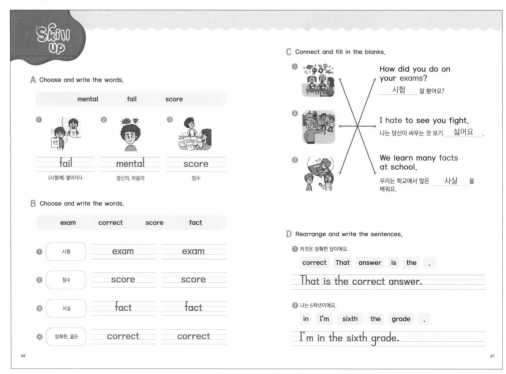

Skill UP

A Choose and write the words.

mental fail score

1. fail — (시험에) 떨어지다
2. mental — 정신의, 마음의
3. score — 점수

B Choose and write the words.

exam correct score fact

1. 시험 — exam — exam
2. 점수 — score — score
3. 사실 — fact — fact
4. 정확한, 옳은 — correct — correct

C Connect and fill in the blanks.

1. How did you do on your exams?
   __시험__ 잘 봤어요?
2. I hate to see you fight.
   나는 당신이 싸우는 것 보기 __싫어요__ .
3. We learn many facts at school.
   우리는 학교에서 많은 __사실__ 을 배워요.

D Rearrange and write the sentences.

1. 저것은 정확한 답이에요.
   correct That answer is the .
   __That is the correct answer.__
2. 나는 6학년이에요.
   in I'm sixth the grade .
   __I'm in the sixth grade.__

66

67

Day 10

P69

 ✓ 여행 ☐ 풍경 ✓ 시골 지역 ☐ 혼자

P72~73

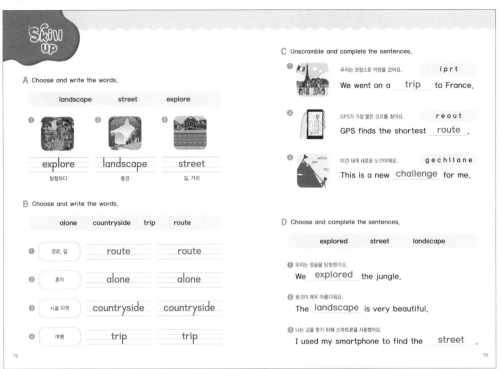

A Choose and write the words.

landscape　street　explore

① explore 탐험하다
② landscape 풍경
③ street 길, 거리

B Choose and write the words.

alone　countryside　trip　route

① 경로, 길　route　route
② 혼자　alone　alone
③ 시골 지역　countryside　countryside
④ 여행　trip　trip

C Unscramble and complete the sentences.

① 우리는 프랑스로 여행을 갔어요.　i p r t
We went on a **trip** to France.

② GPS가 가장 짧은 경로를 찾아요.　r e o u t
GPS finds the shortest **route**.

③ 이건 내게 새로운 도전이에요.　g e c h l l a n e
This is a new **challenge** for me.

D Choose and complete the sentences.

explored　street　landscape

① 우리는 정글을 탐험했어요.
We **explored** the jungle.

② 풍경이 매우 아름다워요.
The **landscape** is very beautiful.

③ 나는 길을 찾기 위해 스마트폰을 사용했어요.
I used my smartphone to find the **street**.

Day 06~10

P74

P76

Day 11

Pop Quiz □ 가게 ✓ 코미디 ✓ 식당 □ 극장

Skill UP

A Find, circle, and write the words.

① o l(shop)i e
가게 **shop**

② t r a(after)c
(시간상으로) 뒤에, 후에 **after**

③ a u(before)
(시간상으로) 전에, 앞에 **before**

④ (comed)y c t
코미디, 희극 **comedy**

B Cross out, unscramble, and write the words.

① 식당 e a a t r u n t s r ⊗ **restaurant**

② 극장 ⊗ h t t r e a e **theater**

③ 끔찍한, 형편없는 r r i t ⊗ b e l e **terrible**

④ 특별한 ⊗ l i p s c e a **special**

C Connect and fill in the blanks.

① We went to an Italian restaurant.
우리는 이탈리안 식당 에 갔어요.

② I like to watch comedies.
나는 코미디 보는 것을 좋아해요.

③ I have special plans for this weekend.
나는 이번 주말에 특별한 계획이 있어요.

D Rearrange and write the sentences.

① 그것은 끔찍한 사고였어요.
a was It accident terrible .
It was a terrible accident.

② 우리는 저녁 식사 이후 떠날 거예요.
leave We'll dinner after .
We'll leave after dinner.

82   83

Day 12

Pop Quiz ✓ 콘서트 □ 영화관 ✓ 중앙, 가운데의 □ 앞쪽의, 앞면

Skill UP

A Choose and write the words.

| middle | sound | concert |

① **concert**
콘서트, 연주회

② **sound**
소리, 연주

③ **middle**
중앙, 가운데의

B Choose and write the words.

| cinema | row | depend | front |

① 영화관 **cinema** **cinema**

② 앞쪽의, 앞면 **front** **front**

③ (극장 등의 좌석) 줄 **row** **row**

④ ~에 달려 있다, 좌우되다 **depend** **depend**

C Connect and fill in the blanks.

① I can see him on the screen.
그를 화면 에서 볼 수 있어요.

② I was sitting in the second row.
나는 두 번째 줄 에 앉아 있었어요.

③ Why don't we go to the cinema tonight?
오늘 밤 영화관 에 가지 않을래요?

D Rearrange and write the sentences.

① 나는 그들의 연주가 좋아요.
sound like their I .
I like their sound.

② 그녀의 첫 콘서트는 대성공이었어요.
sucess first concert is a great Her .
Her first concert is a great success.

88   89

Day 13

P91

 **Pop Quiz** ☑ 팔다 ☐ 확인하다 ☑ 거울 ☐ 현금

P94~95

Skill UP

A Choose and write the words.

| mirror | price | customer |

❶ customer
손님, 고객

❷ mirror
거울

❸ price
가격

B Choose and write the words.

| sell | goods | check | cash |

❶ 팔다 — sell / sell
❷ 현금, 돈 — cash / cash
❸ 확인하다 — check / check
❹ 상품 — goods / goods

C Unscramble and complete the sentences.

❶ 그 가게는 유기농 제품을 팔아요. llses
The store sells some organic products.

❷ 현금을 얼마나 가지고 계시나요? ahcs
How much cash do you have?

❸ 쇼핑 목록을 확인해 보세요. cekhC
Check your shopping list.

D Choose and complete the sentences.

| slide | mirror | goods |

❶ 내 여동생은 거울을 들여다보고 있어요.
My sister is looking in the mirror.

❷ 그 가게에는 많은 상품이 있어요.
There are a lot of goods in the store.

❸ 장난감 가게에는 큰 미끄럼틀이 있어요.
The toy store has a big slide.

94 / 95

Day 14

P97

Pop Quiz ☑ 수도 ☐ 궁전 ☑ 구조물 ☐ 땅

P100~101

Skill UP

A Find, circle, and write the words.

❶ ol e live n → live
살다

❷ l a palace n → palace
궁전

❸ n capital → capital
수도

❹ address → address
주소,
주소를 쓰다

B Cross out, unscramble, and write the words.

❶ 다리 — debrigx → bridge
❷ 땅 — alxnd → land
❸ 구조, 구조물 — streurtcxu → structure
❹ 자원 — rxreuseco → resource

C Connect and fill in the blanks.

❶ The land is located in the south.
그 땅 은 남쪽에 위치해 있어요.

❷ A stone bridge crosses the stream.
를 다리 가 시내를 가로질러요.

❸ The structure of this building is complicated.
이 건물은 구조 가 복잡해요.

D Rearrange and write the sentences.

❶ 나는 런던에 살아요.
in I London live .
I live in London.

❷ 이 건물의 주소는 무엇인가요?
building's What address is this ?
What is this building's address?

100 / 101

Day 15

P103

 Pop Quiz ✓ 도착하다 ☐ 들어가다 ☐ 사실인 ✓ 무료의

P106~107

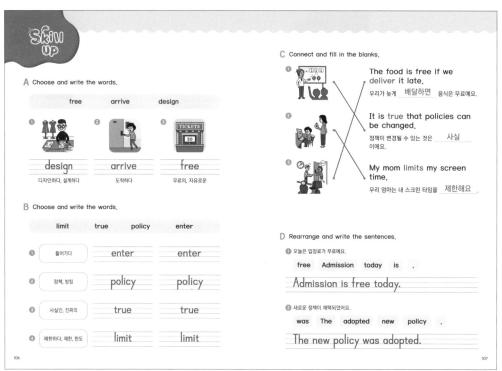

Skill UP

A Choose and write the words.

| free | arrive | design |

① design — 디자인하다, 설계하다
② arrive — 도착하다
③ free — 무료의, 자유로운

B Choose and write the words.

| limit | true | policy | enter |

① 들어가다	enter	enter
② 정책, 방침	policy	policy
③ 사실인, 진짜의	true	true
④ 제한하다, 제한, 한도	limit	limit

C Connect and fill in the blanks.

① The food is free if we deliver it late.
우리가 늦게 배달하면 음식은 무료예요.

② It is true that policies can be changed.
정책이 변경될 수 있는 것은 사실이에요.

③ My mom limits my screen time.
우리 엄마는 내 스크린 타임을 제한해요.

D Rearrange and write the sentences.

① 오늘은 입장료가 무료예요.
free Admission today is .
Admission is free today.

② 새로운 정책이 채택되었어요.
was The adopted new policy .
The new policy was adopted.

Day 11~15

P108

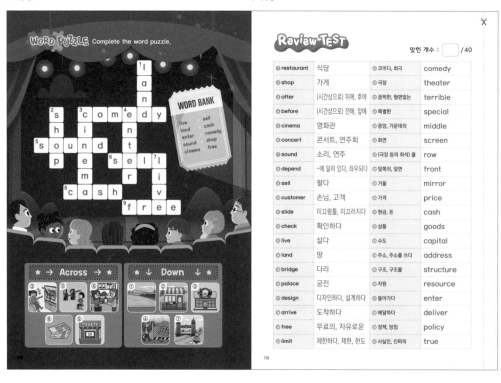

WORD PUZZLE Complete the word puzzle.

P110

Review TEST 맞힌 개수 : ___ / 40

① restaurant	식당	코미디, 희극	comedy
② shop	가게	극장	theater
③ after	(시간상으로) 뒤에, 후에	끔찍한, 형편없는	terrible
④ before	(시간상으로) 전에, 앞에	특별한	special
⑤ cinema	영화관	중앙, 가운데의	middle
⑥ concert	콘서트, 연주회	화면	screen
⑦ sound	소리, 연주	(극장 등의 좌석) 줄	row
⑧ depend	~에 달려 있다, 좌우되다	앞쪽의, 앞면	front
⑨ sell	팔다	거울	mirror
⑩ customer	손님, 고객	가격	price
⑪ slide	미끄럼틀, 미끄러지다	현금, 돈	cash
⑫ check	확인하다	상품	goods
⑬ live	살다	수도	capital
⑭ land	땅	주소, 주소를 쓰다	address
⑮ bridge	다리	구조, 구조물	structure
⑯ palace	궁전	자원	resource
⑰ design	디자인하다, 설계하다	들어가다	enter
⑱ arrive	도착하다	배달하다	deliver
⑲ free	무료의, 자유로운	정책, 방침	policy
⑳ limit	제한하다, 제한, 한도	사실인, 진짜의	true

Day 16

P113

 PoP Quiz ☐ 인종 ✓ 인간 ✓ 진화하다 ☐ 관련시키다

P116~117

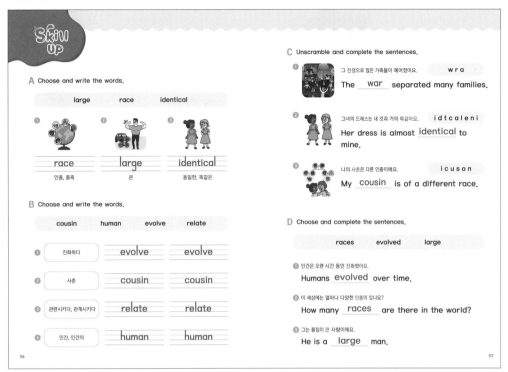

A Choose and write the words.

large	race	identical

① race
인종, 종족

② large
큰

③ identical
동일한, 똑같은

B Choose and write the words.

cousin	human	evolve	relate

① 진화하다 — evolve / evolve

② 사촌 — cousin / cousin

③ 관련시키다, 관계시키다 — relate / relate

④ 인간, 인간의 — human / human

C Unscramble and complete the sentences.

① 그 전쟁으로 많은 가족들이 헤어졌어요.   w r a
The __war__ separated many families.

② 그녀의 드레스는 내 것과 거의 똑같아요.   i d t c a l e n i
Her dress is almost __identical__ to mine.

③ 나의 사촌은 다른 인종이에요.   i c u s o n
My __cousin__ is of a different race.

D Choose and complete the sentences.

races	evolved	large

① 인간은 오랜 시간 동안 진화했어요.
Humans __evolved__ over time.

② 이 세상에는 얼마나 다양한 인종이 있나요?
How many __races__ are there in the world?

③ 그는 몸집이 큰 사람이에요.
He is a __large__ man.

116   117

Day 17

P119

 **PoP Quiz** ✓ 식료품 ☐ 저울 ☐ 목록 ✓ 카트

P122~123

A Find, circle, and write the words.

① scaleirt
저울   scale

② groceryb
식료품   grocery

③ vdnearzi
가까운, 가까이   near

④ uylinexz
줄, 선   line

C Connect and fill in the blanks.

① My dad is pushing a cart.
우리 아빠가 __카트__ 를 밀고 있어요.

② Let me weigh the bananas.
바나나 __무게를 달아__ 볼게요.

③ Write a list of the food we need.
우리에게 필요한 음식 __목록__ 을 작성하세요.

B Cross out, unscramble, and write the words.

① 카트   axcrt   cart

② 밀다   sphxu   push

③ 무게를 달다   ehigxw   weigh

④ 목록, 리스트   lxsti   list

D Rearrange and write the sentences.

① 이 줄은 현금만 받아요.
line only cash This is .
This line is cash only.

② 그 시장은 우리 집에서 가까워요.
near house is my The market .
The market is near my house.

122   123

Day 18

P125

Pop Quiz [ ] 깊은 [✓] 거대한   [ ] 어린 [✓] 얕은

P128~129

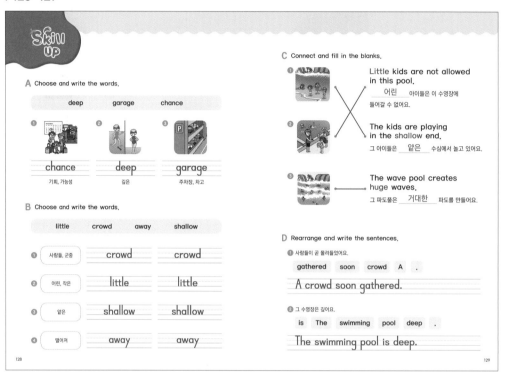

Skill up

A Choose and write the words.

| deep | garage | chance |

❶ chance
기회, 가능성

❷ deep
깊은

❸ garage
주차장, 차고

B Choose and write the words.

| little | crowd | away | shallow |

❶ 사람들, 군중 — crowd — crowd

❷ 어린, 작은 — little — little

❸ 얕은 — shallow — shallow

❹ 떨어져 — away — away

C Connect and fill in the blanks.

❶ Little kids are not allowed in this pool.
어린 아이들은 이 수영장에 들어갈 수 없어요.

❷ The kids are playing in the shallow end.
그 아이들은 얕은 수심에서 놀고 있어요.

❸ The wave pool creates huge waves.
그 파도풀은 거대한 파도를 만들어요.

D Rearrange and write the sentences.

❶ 사람들이 곧 몰려들었어요.

| gathered | soon | crowd | A | . |

A crowd soon gathered.

❷ 그 수영장은 깊어요.

| is | The | swimming | pool | deep | . |

The swimming pool is deep.

128   129

Day 19

P131

Pop Quiz [✓] 거의 [ ] 물건   [ ] 피부 [✓] 목표

P134~135

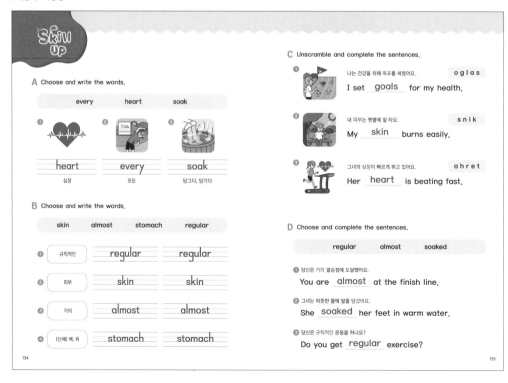

Skill up

A Choose and write the words.

| every | heart | soak |

❶ heart
심장

❷ every
모든

❸ soak
담그다, 담기다

B Choose and write the words.

| skin | almost | stomach | regular |

❶ 규칙적인 — regular — regular

❷ 피부 — skin — skin

❸ 거의 — almost — almost

❹ (신체) 배, 위 — stomach — stomach

C Unscramble and complete the sentences.

❶ 나는 건강을 위해 목표를 세웠어요.   o g l a s
I set goals for my health.

❷ 내 피부는 햇볕에 잘 타요.   s n i k
My skin burns easily.

❸ 그녀의 심장이 빠르게 뛰고 있어요.   a h r e t
Her heart is beating fast.

D Choose and complete the sentences.

| regular | almost | soaked |

❶ 당신은 거의 결승점에 도달했어요.
You are almost at the finish line.

❷ 그녀는 따뜻한 물에 발을 담갔어요.
She soaked her feet in warm water.

❸ 당신은 규칙적인 운동을 하나요?
Do you get regular exercise?

134   135

P137

  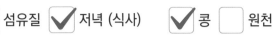

☐ 섬유질　☑ 저녁 (식사)　☑ 콩　☐ 원천

P140~141

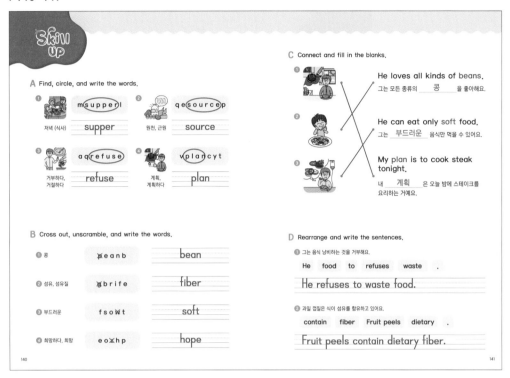

Day 16~20

P142　　　　　　　　　　　　　　　P144

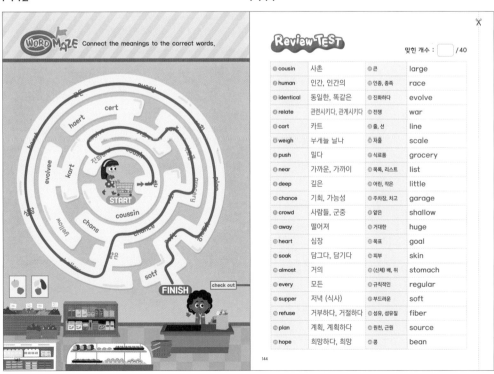

Day 21

P147

 ☐ 출구 ☑ 항공편 ☑ 좌석 ☐ 엔진

P150~151

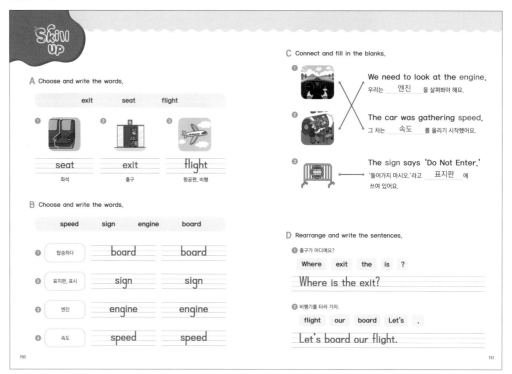

Skill UP

A Choose and write the words.

| exit | seat | flight |

① seat (좌석)
② exit (출구)
③ flight (항공편, 비행)

B Choose and write the words.

| speed | sign | engine | board |

① 탑승하다 — board board
② 표지판, 표시 — sign sign
③ 엔진 — engine engine
④ 속도 — speed speed

C Connect and fill in the blanks.

① We need to look at the engine.
우리는 엔진 을 살펴봐야 해요.

② The car was gathering speed.
그 차는 속도 를 올리기 시작했어요.

③ The sign says 'Do Not Enter.'
'들어가지 마시오.'라고 표지판 에 쓰여 있어요.

D Rearrange and write the sentences.

① 출구가 어디예요?
Where | exit | the | is | ?
Where is the exit?

② 비행기를 타러 가자.
flight | our | board | Let's | .
Let's board our flight.

150   151

Day 22

P153

☑ 전에 ☐ 일주일 ☐ 혜택 ☑ 휴식

P156~157

Skill UP

A Choose and write the words.

| rest | benefit | blood |

① benefit (혜택, 이점)
② rest (휴식, 쉬다)
③ blood (피, 혈액)

B Choose and write the words.

| type | week | collect | donate |

① 일주일, 주 — week week
② 모으다 — collect collect
③ 종류, 유형 — type type
④ 기부하다, 기증하다 — donate donate

C Unscramble and complete the sentences.

① 당신은 휴식을 취해야 해요.   rtse
You should take a rest .

② 당신의 혈액형은 무엇이예요?   ptey
What is your blood type ?

③ 그녀는 매주 도서관에서 봉사 활동을 해요.   kwee
She volunteers at the library every week .

D Choose and complete the sentences.

| collect | ago | benefits |

① 나는 2년 전에 동물들을 돌보는 것을 도왔어요.
I helped take care of animals two years ago .

② 그들은 가난한 사람들을 위해 옷을 모아요.
They collect clothes for the poor.

③ 봉사 활동에는 많은 이점이 있어요.
There are many benefits to volunteer work.

156   157

Day 23

P159

Pop Quiz
 ☑ 높은 ☐ 멀리 ☐ 가능한 ☑ 오르다

P162~163

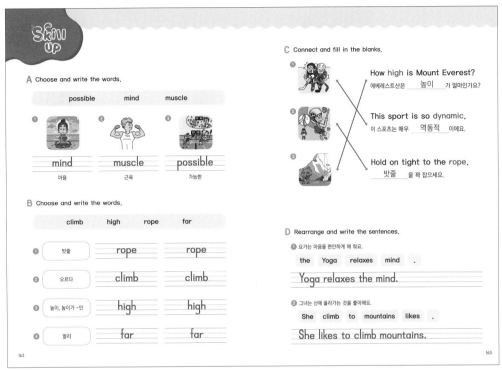

Skill Up

A Choose and write the words.

possible   mind   muscle

1. mind (마음)
2. muscle (근육)
3. possible (가능한)

B Choose and write the words.

climb   high   rope   far

1. 밧줄 — rope / rope
2. 오르다 — climb / climb
3. 높이, 높이가 ~인 — high / high
4. 멀리 — far / far

C Connect and fill in the blanks.

1. How high is Mount Everest?
에베레스트산은 높이 가 얼마인가요?

2. This sport is so dynamic.
이 스포츠는 매우 역동적 이에요.

3. Hold on tight to the rope.
밧줄 을 꽉 잡으세요.

D Rearrange and write the sentences.

1. 요가는 마음을 편안하게 해 줘요.
the Yoga relaxes mind .
Yoga relaxes the mind.

2. 그녀는 산에 올라가는 것을 좋아해요.
She climb to mountains likes .
She likes to climb mountains.

162   163

Day 24

P165

Pop Quiz
☑ 혀 ☐ 꼬리 ☑ 아주 작은 ☐ 거친

P168~169

Skill Up

A Choose and write the words.

dolphin   fox   bone

1. fox (여우)
2. bone (뼈)
3. dolphin (돌고래)

B Choose and write the words.

tail   rough   copy   tongue

1. 꼬리 — tail / tail
2. 혀 — tongue / tongue
3. 거친 — rough / rough
4. 따라 하다, 복사하다 — copy / copy

C Unscramble and complete the sentences.

1. 숲에 여우가 있어요.
o x f
There is a fox in the forest.

2. 개가 꼬리를 흔들고 있어요.
l t a i
A dog is wagging its tail.

3. 그 피부는 딱딱하고 거칠어요.
o g r h u
It has a hard and rough skin.

D Choose and complete the sentences.

bone   tiny   dolphin

1. 그 사슴은 다리뼈가 부러졌어요.
The deer has broken a bone in its leg.

2. 돌고래는 영리한 동물이에요.
The dolphin is an intelligent animal.

3. 새끼 고양이의 발은 아주 작아요.
The kitten's feet are so tiny.

168   169

P171

 ✓ 단단한 ☐ 밝은 ✓ 긴장을 풀다 ☐ 향상시키다

P174~175

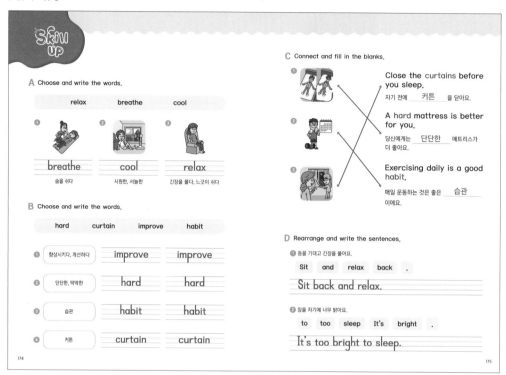

Skill Up

A Choose and write the words.

| relax | breathe | cool |

① breathe
숨을 쉬다

② cool
시원한, 서늘한

③ relax
긴장을 풀다, 느긋이 쉬다

B Choose and write the words.

| hard | curtain | improve | habit |

① 향상시키다, 개선하다 → improve improve

② 단단한, 딱딱한 → hard hard

③ 습관 → habit habit

④ 커튼 → curtain curtain

C Connect and fill in the blanks.

① Close the curtains before you sleep.
자기 전에 커튼 을 닫아요.

② A hard mattress is better for you.
당신에게는 단단한 매트리스가 더 좋아요.

③ Exercising daily is a good habit.
매일 운동하는 것은 좋은 습관 이에요.

D Rearrange and write the sentences.

① 등을 기대고 긴장을 풀어요.
Sit and relax back .
Sit back and relax.

② 잠을 자기에 너무 밝아요.
to too sleep It's bright .
It's too bright to sleep.

174

175

P176

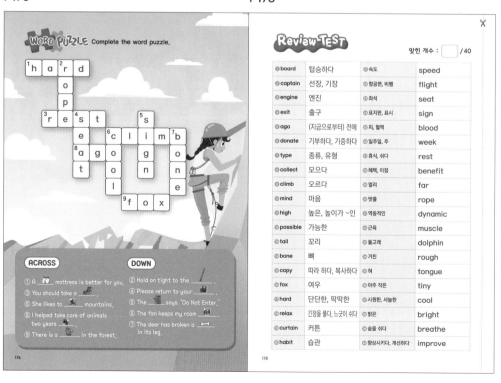

WORD PUZZLE Complete the word puzzle.

¹h a ²r d
³r e s t ⁵s
⁶c l i m ⁷b
⁸a g o g o
 n l n
 ⁹f o x

ACROSS
① A ___ mattress is better for you.
③ You should take a ___.
⑤ She likes to ___ mountains.
⑧ I helped take care of animals two years ___.
⑨ There is a ___ in the forest.

DOWN
② Hold on tight to the ___.
④ Please return to your ___.
⑤ The ___ says 'Do Not Enter.'
⑥ The fan keeps my room ___.
⑦ The deer has broken a ___ in its leg.

176

P178

Review Test

맞힌 개수 : ___ / 40

① board	탑승하다	⑩ 속도	speed
② captain	선장, 기장	⑫ 항공편, 비행	flight
③ engine	엔진	⑬ 좌석	seat
④ exit	출구	⑭ 표지판, 표시	sign
⑤ ago	(지금으로부터) 전에	⑮ 피, 혈액	blood
⑥ donate	기부하다, 기증하다	⑯ 일주일, 주	week
⑦ type	종류, 유형	⑰ 휴식, 쉬다	rest
⑧ collect	모으다	⑱ 혜택, 이점	benefit
⑨ climb	오르다	⑲ 멀리	far
⑩ mind	마음	⑳ 밧줄	rope
⑪ high	높은, 높이가 ~인	㉑ 역동적인	dynamic
⑫ possible	가능한	㉒ 근육	muscle
⑬ tail	꼬리	㉓ 돌고래	dolphin
⑭ bone	뼈	㉔ 거친	rough
⑮ copy	따라 하다, 복사하다	㉕ 혀	tongue
⑯ fox	여우	㉖ 아주 작은	tiny
⑰ hard	단단한, 딱딱한	㉗ 시원한, 서늘한	cool
⑱ relax	긴장을 풀다, 느긋이 쉬다	㉘ 밝은	bright
⑲ curtain	커튼	㉙ 숨을 쉬다	breathe
⑳ habit	습관	㉚ 향상시키다, 개선하다	improve

178

Word List

a

address	주소, 주소를 쓰다
after	(시간상으로) 뒤에, 후에
ago	(지금으로부터) 전에
almost	거의
alone	혼자
around	~ 주위에, 주변에
arrive	도착하다
aunt	이모, 고모, 숙모
available	구할 수 있는
away	떨어져

b

bean	콩
before	(시간상으로) 전에, 앞에
believe	믿다
benefit	혜택, 이점
bite	물다
blood	피, 혈액
board	탑승하다
bone	뼈
bowl	그릇
brain	두뇌, 뇌
breathe	숨을 쉬다
bridge	다리
bright	밝은
bury	묻다, 매장하다

c

capital	수도
captain	선장, 기장
cart	카트
cash	현금, 돈
cave	동굴
challenge	도전, 도전하다
chance	기회, 가능성
check	확인하다
church	교회
cinema	영화관
climb	오르다
close	가까운
clue	단서
collect	모으다

comedy	코미디, 희극
concert	콘서트, 연주회
confuse	혼동하다
consume	소모하다, 소비하다
control	조절하다, 통제
cool	시원한, 서늘한
copy	따라 하다, 복사하다
correct	정확한, 옳은
countryside	시골 지역
cousin	사촌
crowd	사람들, 군중
culture	문화
curtain	커튼
customer	손님, 고객

d

death	죽음
declare	선언하다
deep	깊은
deliver	배달하다
depend	~에 달려 있다, 좌우되다
design	디자인하다, 설계하다
different	다른
difficult	어려운
dolphin	돌고래
donate	기부하다, 기증하다
dot	점

e

Earth	지구
easy	쉬운
engine	엔진
enough	충분한
enter	들어가다
every	모든
evolve	진화하다
exam	시험
exit	출구
explore	탐험하다

f

fact	사실
fail	(시험에) 떨어지다

far	멀리
feed	먹이를 주다
fiber	섬유질, 섬유
field	들판
flight	항공편, 비행
forest	숲
formal	격식을 차린, 정중한
fox	여우
free	무료의, 자유로운
front	앞쪽의, 앞면
funeral	장례식

g

gain	얻다, 늘리다
garage	주차장, 차고
goal	목표
goods	상품
grade	학년, 성적
grandfather	할아버지
grave	산소, 무덤
grocery	식료품
ground	땅

h

habit	습관
hard	단단한, 딱딱한
hate	몹시 싫어하다
heart	심장
high	높은, 높이가 ~인
hobby	취미
hope	희망하다, 희망
huge	거내한
human	인간, 인간의
hunt	사냥하다

i

identical	동일한, 똑같은
improve	향쪽시키다, 개선하다

k

keep	유지하다, 가지고 있다

l

land	땅
landscape	풍경
large	큰
leaf	나뭇잎
limit	제한하다, 제한, 한도
line	줄, 선
list	목록, 리스트
little	어린, 작은
live	살다
lose	줄다, 잃다
low	낮은

m

memory	기억(력)
mental	정신의, 마음의
middle	중앙, 가운데의
mind	마음
mirror	거울
mouse	쥐
muscle	근육

n

near	가까운, 가까이

o

ocean	바다, 대양
one	하나, 하나의
order	주문하다, 주문

p

palace	궁전
pet	반려동물
plan	계획, 계획하다
planet	행성
policy	정책, 방침
possible	가능한
price	가격
primitive	원시의, 원시적인
puppy	강아지
push	밀다
puzzle	퍼즐, 수수께끼

r

race	인종, 종족
refuse	거부하다, 거절하다
regular	규칙적인
relate	관련시키다, 관계시키다
relative	친척
relax	긴장을 풀다, 느긋이 쉬다
relieve	없애 주다, 완화하다
resource	자원
responsible	책임감 있는
rest	휴식, 쉬다
restaurant	식당
rope	밧줄
rough	거친
route	경로, 길
row	(극장 등의 좌석) 줄

s

same	같은
scale	저울
score	점수
screen	화면
seat	좌석
sell	팔다
shallow	얕은
shop	가게
side	(좌우 절반 중 한) 쪽
sign	표지판, 표시
skin	피부
slide	미끄럼틀, 미끄러지다
slim	날씬한
soak	담그다, 담기다
soft	부드러운
sound	소리, 연주
source	원천, 근원
space	우주
special	특별한
speed	속도
stomach	(신체) 배, 위
straight	곧은, 똑바른
street	길, 거리
structure	구조, 구조물
supper	저녁 (식사)
surface	표면
survive	살아남다

t

tail	꼬리
terrible	끔찍한, 형편없는
theater	극장
thin	마른, 얇은
tiny	아주 작은
tongue	혀
trip	여행
twin	쌍둥이
type	종류, 유형
true	사실인, 진짜의

u

uncle	삼촌, 이모부, 고모부

w

war	전쟁
wedding	결혼식
week	일주일, 주
weigh	무게를 달다
wild	야생, 야생의